The Virtues Unveiled

The Virtues Unveiled

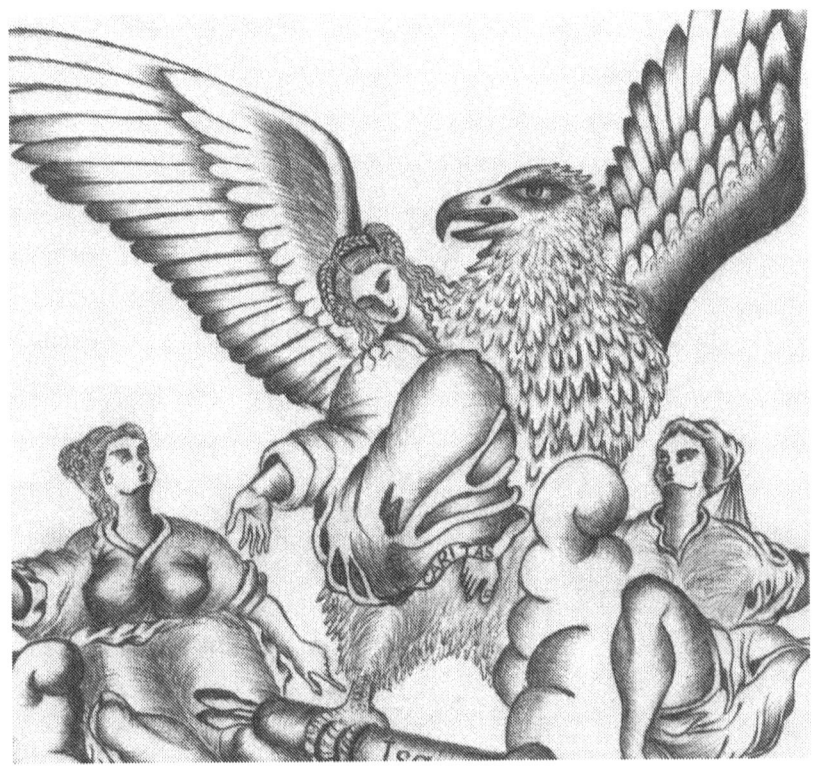

Joseph E. Ssali

Illustrated by the author

iUniverse, Inc.

New York Lincoln Shanghai

The Virtues Unveiled

iUniverse, Inc.

For information address:
iUniverse
2021 Pine Lake Road, Suite 100
Lincoln, NE 68512
www.iuniverse.com

A Graph-X Media Production. Graph-X Media is a division of
Mp3joseph.com.

ISBN: 0-595-28236-9 (Pbk)
ISBN: 0-595-74750-7 (Cloth)

Printed in the United States of America

A Personal Word

The first major project I undertook was this inspirational book–*The Virtues Unveiled*. For a very long time, I avoided the arts and pursued the Sciences, but within me was a fire for the arts that I was unable to quench. After several years, I finally relented and wrote then illustrated my first book, *The Virtues Unveiled*.

When I worked on this book, I realized that I needed illustrations to accompany the text. It was then that I prayed earnestly to God for divine inspiration, to enable me to draw illustrations that would do justice to the glory of His name. It was such an experience putting the whole project together, and upon completion, I felt a deep sense of gratification that the soul wouldn't wish to lose.

-Joseph E. Ssali

Contents

PART I

The Celebration Of The Virtues
Illustrated by the author in black-ink pen

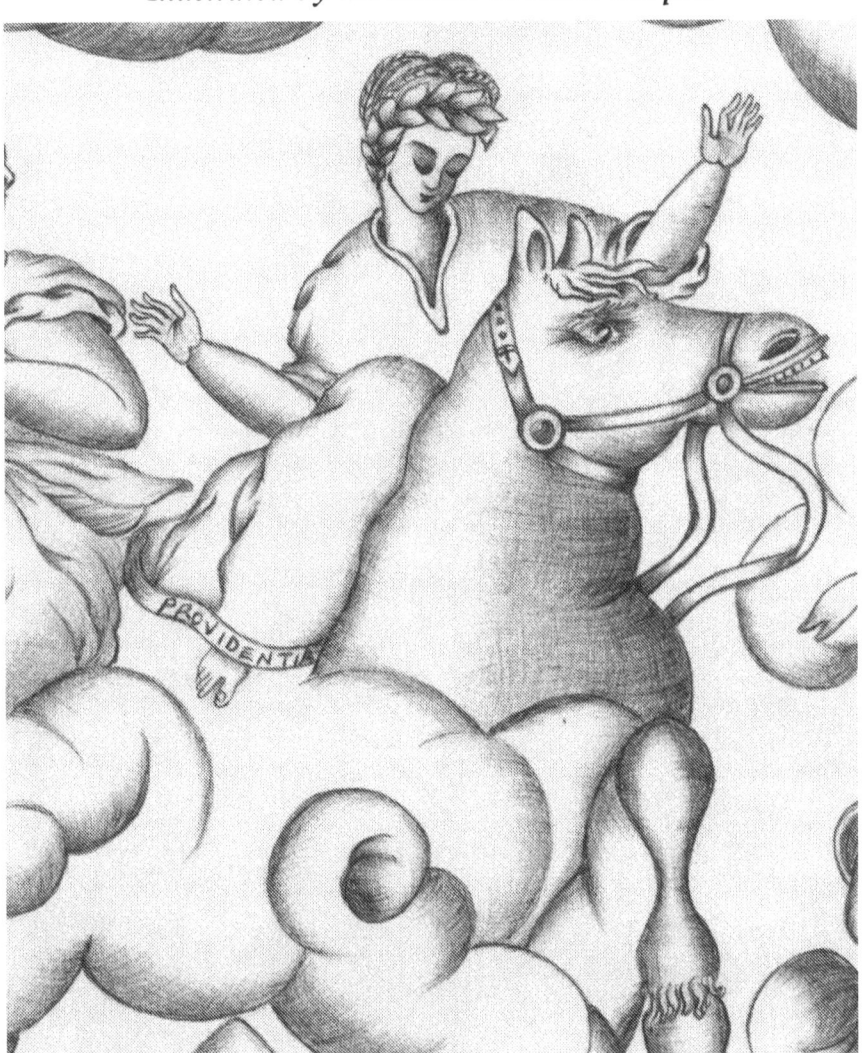

The purpose of virtues is to regulate the conduct of man. Originally emphasis was put mainly on four of the virtues which are: Prudence, Fortitude, Temperance and Justice. Later on Gregory the Great was inspired by a letter written by St. Paul to the inhabitants of the ancient city of Corinth, so the last three of the seven virtues were then added. These are; Faith, Hope, and Charity.

In this book I have also added five more, which are derivatives of the seven virtues. I have included Providence, Wisdom, Truth, Grace and Mercy. Divine Providence, Divine Wisdom, and Divine Love are so intertwined, you cannot mention one without mentioning the other. In this book all my artwork is in themes and is very allegorical. The shaping of my artistry was greatly influenced by the words of Giorgio Vasari a sixteenth century biographer and artist who said, "Every artist must be well-balanced, and not excel in one area, at the expense of another." I have since made it a point to pursue balance.

While the Greeks and Renaissance artists celebrated classical antiquity, the Baroque masters created art filled with emotional dynamism and dramatic movement. Their art transcended the laws of nature and often seemed to defy gravity. They solved the problems that had perturbed the Greek and Renaissance masters. The result of the 17th century Baroque was an art that dominated the civilized world and surpassed even their predecessors.

In creating The Virtues Unveiled, I put together an amalgamation of what I have learned from classical antiquity to the Renaissance and the Baroque. In all my renderings I pursue beauty, harmony, and balance. I believe a true artist should be able to portray humans and animals with ease. As far as humans are concerned, an artist should be able to draw both male and female, including old and young with the same kind of ease.

I will give you a step-by-step guide into my work and explain all the themes. One thing you have to bear in mind is that every drawing in this book has a theme behind it. Nothing made it in here by mistake. I will not try to be ambiguous that's why I named this book The Virtues Unveiled. In regard to an artist making a well-balanced representation of an artistic composition, I try to capture that in the first rendering of this book. This is illustrated in *The Triumph Of The Virtues–Youth and Age.*

In this allegorical rendering, we see four of the virtues in the inter- mediate realm. In the center, riding a horse is Divine Providence, and seated to her right is Prudence. To the left of Providence is Fortitude, and beneath her is Temperance who is seen holding a flute. Divine Providence is considered to be one of the cardinal virtues that's why she is riding on a horse above the rest of them.

The virtues here serve as a double compliment. They represent youth, and the horse represents strength that comes along with it. Horses have been used by noblemen and conquerors in battle because of their speed and raw power. In the earthly realm are four male figures. These also serve as a double compliment. First they represent the four Church fathers: Augustine, Athanasius, Ambrose, and John Chysostom–all of whom are saints. Secondly they represent the wisdom that comes with age. This drawing is therefore a celebration of the beauty and strength of youthfulness, and the grace, nobility, and wisdom of age. The four Church fathers each express a different passion of the soul.

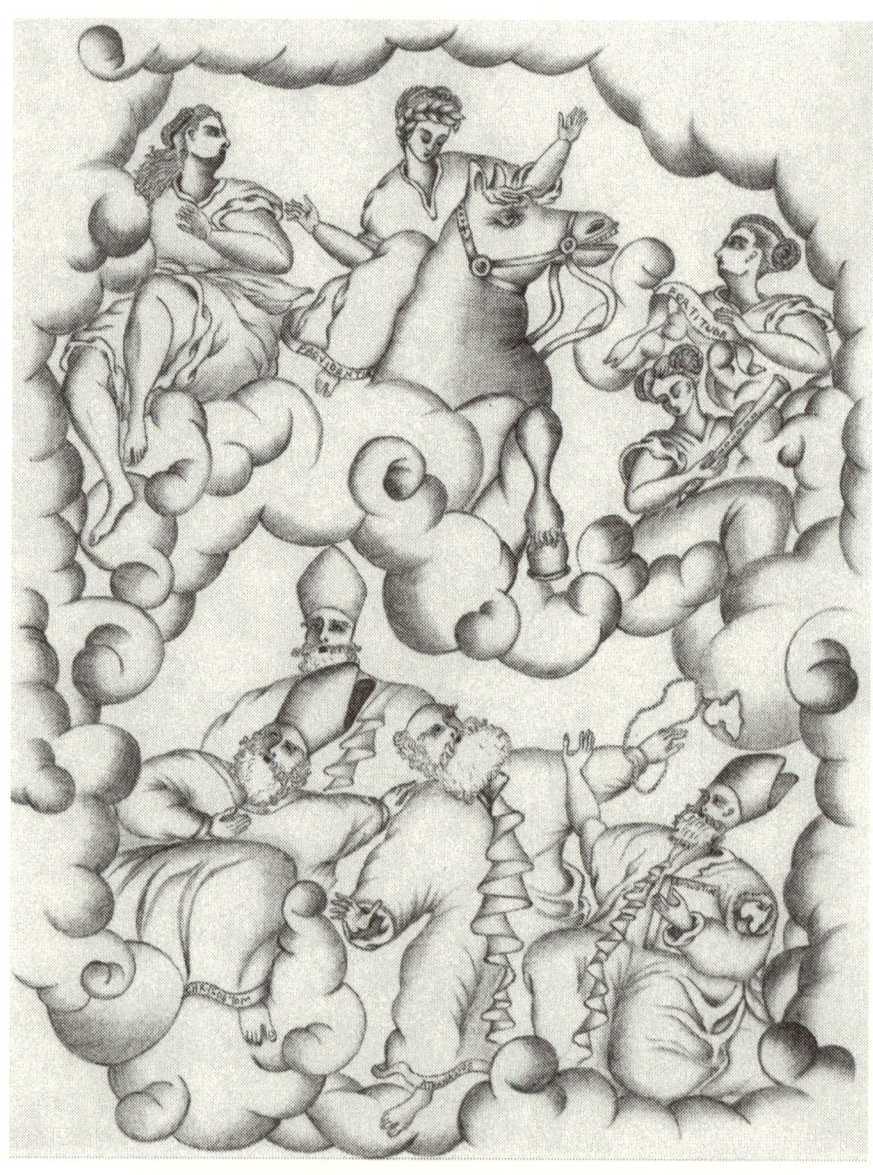

The Triumph Of The Virtues–Youth and Age

All four of these great men have been captivated by The Virtues (*speculum morale*). St. Augustine to the far right is seen carrying a book with some of his writings. He is also kneeling down as a sign of submission to The Virtues. On the left shoulder of Augustine's drapery is a badge of Africa, where he was born in the town of Hippo. Next to him is Athanasius who is awed by The Virtues and is carrying a necklace with the map of the continent hanging on it. Athanasius too was born in North Africa in the city of Alexandria. Both Augustine and Athanasius proudly display these symbols to celebrate their African heritage.

St. John Chrysostom on the far left is leaning on Athanasius and is seen laying his right hand on his breast as a symbol of humility, while the ever so noble Ambrose stares in shocked silence at Prudence. One can only imagine what's going through the mind of Athanasius. As I tried to read his thoughts, I penned down the following lines.

Oh how I wish, my life were faultless…
…but through my own strength, I can't be flawless
    I always yearn, to do what's right
        Yet time and again, I tend to lose sight.

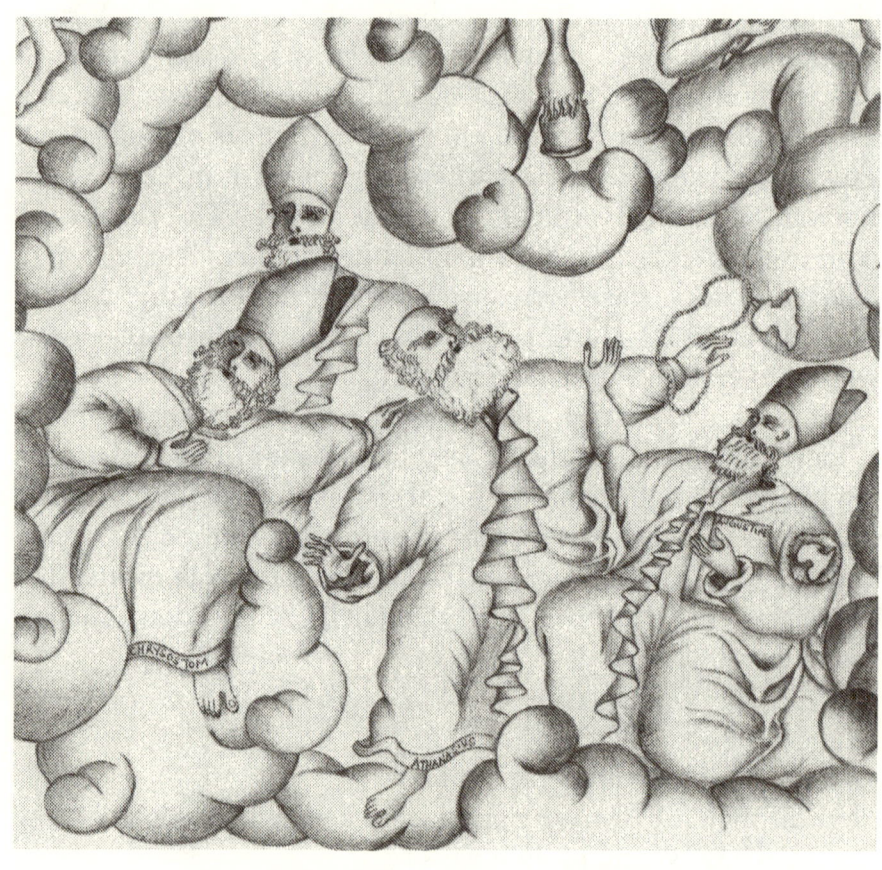

The Four Church Fathers
From left to right-John Chrysostom, Ambrose, Athanasius and Augustine

In *Wisdom and Truth,* Divine Wisdom is shown reading an inscription with the words written by King Solomon about her that say, "**...Love Wisdom, and she will make you great. Embrace her, and she will bring you honor. She will be your crowning glory.**" Truth is playing a tambourine as she marvels while Wisdom reads the beautiful words.

Also included are Dante, and Thomas Aquinas, both of whom were contemporaries and the greatest minds of their day. St. Thomas Aquinas represents Theology and can be seen holding the book of virtues. On the other hand, the youthful Dante represents poetry. Dante is shown gazing at Truth whom he greatly admires and incorporates her in his writings, while Aquinas is gazing toward Wisdom. Truth is not included in the traditional virtues because she is the embodiment of Justice. I will talk about Justice in later chapters of this book.

As for the two cherubim, I realized that the only way the book of Wisdom would remain airborne, is if it were touched by an angel. Divine Wisdom is a sub-set of Divine Providence and has been isolated with Truth in this drawing.

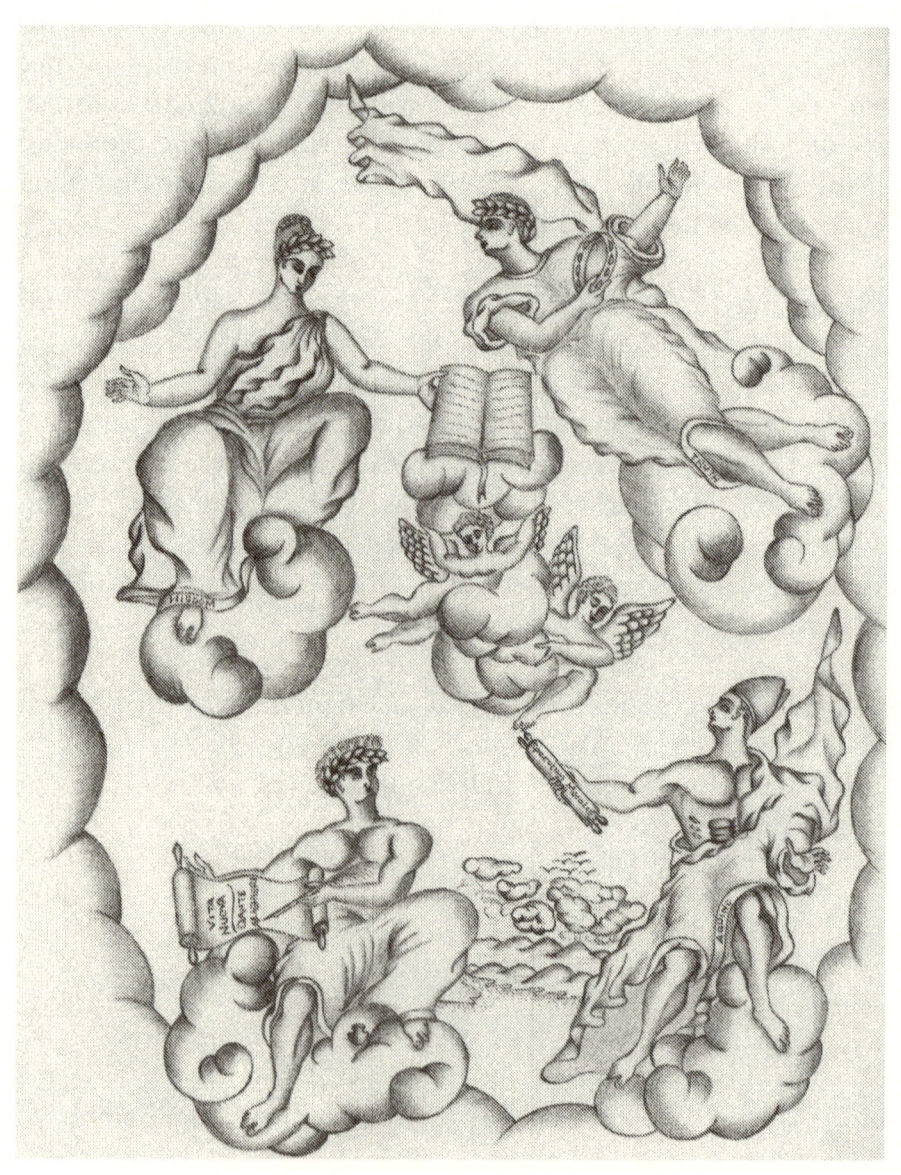

Wisdom and Truth

Dante Alighieri, the Florentine poet is shown here in detail. He is represented as a youth displaying the title of his first great work *Vita Nuova* which means 'New Life.' In this book he tells the story of his love for Beatrice whom he had met as a youth and fallen in love with. Considered to be one of the greatest writers of all time, he eclipsed even the ancient Roman poets in stature. These included Lucretius, famous for *The Nature Of Things,* Virgil (*Pastoral poems*), Ovid (*Metamorphoses*), and Horace (*Odes and verse Epistles*).

It is believed that Dante was influenced by some of the writings of the above-mentioned poets and was familiar with the work of Homer, one of the greatest Greek writers. He later on created work that had a more sacred theme to it as opposed to the mythological and secular works that had been composed by the earlier writers.

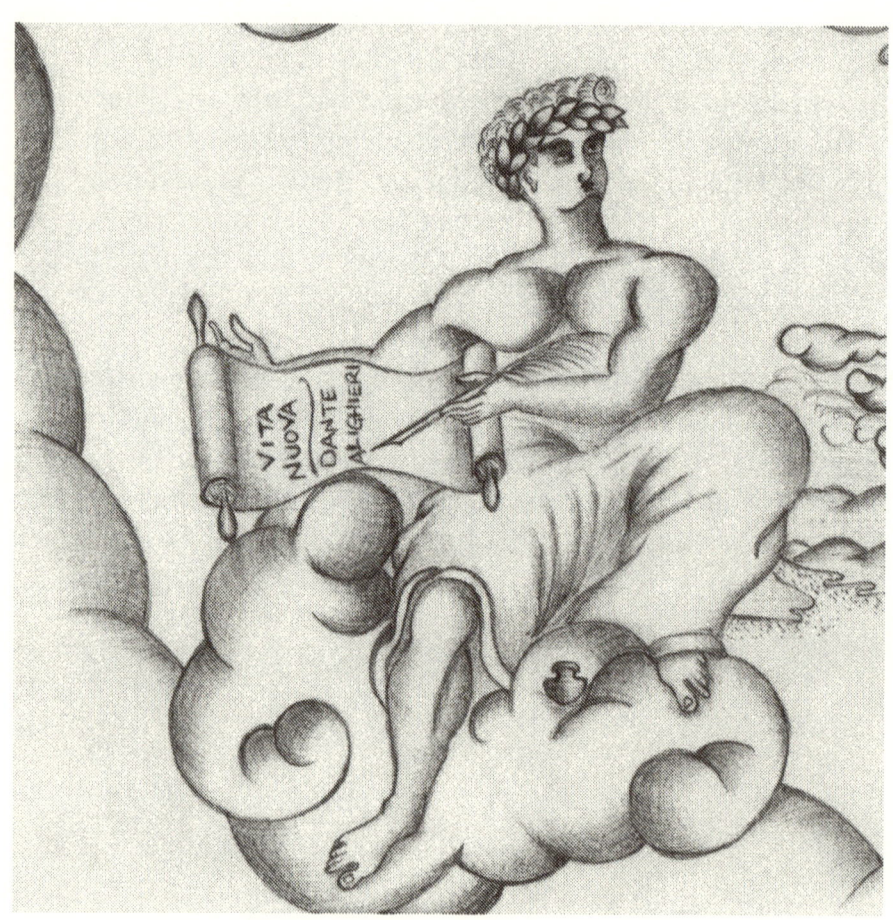

Detail of Dante

Not even heaven can deny the beauty and splendor that Truth embodies. She is one of the most beautiful virtues, and has been isolated in relation with Time. Father Time is shown unveiling Truth (*Veritas*) to reveal her and the beauty she personifies. This allegorical composition was inspired by Bernini's words that; "One must always work with Truth, since in the end she is discovered by Time." As he irresistibly undrapes Truth, the aged Father Time is also shown carrying a globe in his left hand. The globe is symbolic of the earth where Time reigns, for outside the universe, Time ceases to exist-it's eternity. Time has two sides to it. First there is the creative nature, and by this I mean that all things are created within a certain period of time. There is also the destructive nature of time, in that with time, all things deteriorate. The only things that are not affected by time are the ones that are intangible including the virtues.

A few examples are some of the liberal arts, which I also talk about in a later chapter. Two of them are Music and Grammar. Music seems to be able to live on regardless of time. That eternal quality is one of the factors that makes it such a universal language. In respect to Grammar, words too have such power and a sense of timelessness. It was the great Latin poet Horace who said, "...I have built a monument (*words*) that is more permanent than bronze."

The laurel wreath around Truth's head, and the palm bough that she's holding in her left hand celebrate the triumph of Truth (the virtues). The inscription on the base of the scrollwork that reads, "*Veritas Filia Temporis*," simply means, "Truth is the daughter of Time."

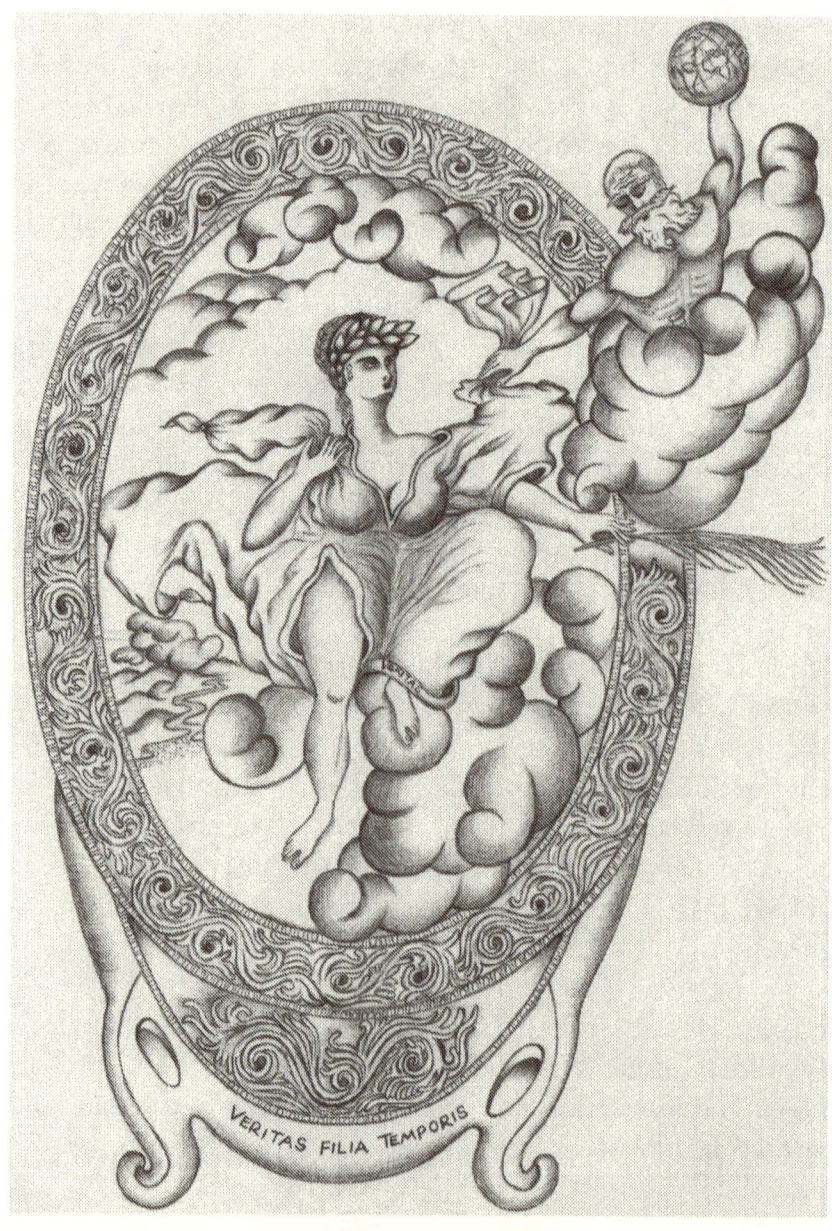

VERITAS FILIA TEMPORIS

Time reveals Truth

This piece shows Grace holding an olive branch in her right hand and Mercy kneeling down. The rendering of Grace and Mercy was inspired by the belief that those who are sincerely remorseful about their vices, yearn to be treated with leniency. Grace and Mercy are by-products of Divine Love, which is one of the seven virtues. Divine Love is comprised of: Grace, Mercy, Clemency and Leniency. In addition to the seven virtues which are: Fortitude (*Fortitudo*), Temperance (*Temperantia*), Prudence (*Prudentia*), Justice (*Justitia*), Faith (*Fides*), Hope (*Spes*), and Divine Love or Charity (*Caritas*), I have included a few more in order to make this work more diversified. Indeed there are a lot more virtues that have not been mentioned in this book, but they all emanate from the seven virtues.

The male figure in this composition is Longinus. Longinus was the Roman centurion who pierced Christ in His side with the Holy Lance. Legend has it that Longinus was partially blind, however, after piercing Jesus Christ in the side, some of the blood mixed with water dropped in the eyes of Longinus. It was then that Longinus miraculously regained his full eyesight, and upon laying his eyes on Christ, he was prompted to make the profound utterance, "…Truly, this man was the Son of God." Longinus was then converted to Christianity and after his death, he was later on canonized into sainthood.

There is a lot of speculation about the whereabouts of the Longinus spear. There is a school of thought that says it is embedded within the confines of St. Peter's Basilica in Rome, and there is another school of thought that says the Holy Lance is in one of the prominent European museums. In this book, Longinus is holding the Holy Lance in his left hand.

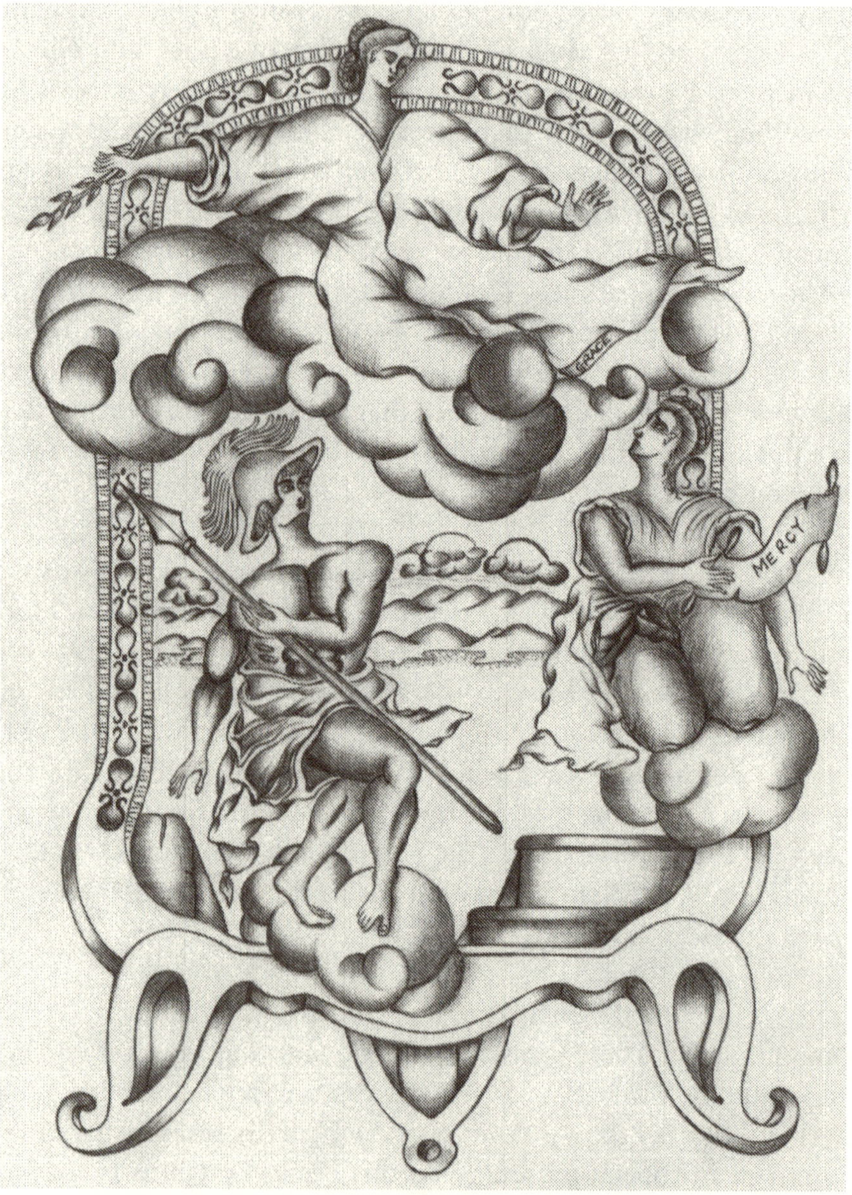

Grace and Mercy–Mea Culpa

In this detailed picture of Longinus, he has a 'Caeser hair-cut' which would only have been appropriate for a man of his stature. He is also standing with the *contrapposto* (counter-pose) to suggest movement. The counter-pose is where one part of the body is twisted in a direction opposite the other. This standard again goes back to classical antiquity and the Greeks used it a lot in their sculpture to add dramatic movement to the statues. One good example is the statue of Lacoön and his two sons. The mythological tale behind the skillfully carved group, is that while Laocoön was offering a bull as a sacrifice to one of the Greek gods, two serpents came out of the sea and killed him and his two sons.

This rule in art (*contrapposto*) was then adopted by the Renaissance artists and was later on perfected by the Baroque masters in the 17th century who used it in sculpture and their paintings. The greatest example is the work of the founder of Baroque, the great GianLorenzo Bernini. He was a courtier, a painter, sculptor, poet, architect, musician, an engineer, and an excellent raconteur. To Bernini even speech was an art form. He spoke so beautifully that the pope (Maffeo Baberini) also referred to as Urban VIII, required the impresario to tell him a story every night before he went to bed. In all his work, he pursued excellence and is perhaps the greatest artist of all time. My life changed when I first encountered his work. It's almost as if the hand of God had been placed upon Bernini's hand while he was creating his work. No other artist achieved the accomplishments that Bernini did. Even his portrait busts seem to exude movement and life. It is said that after Bernini had finished carving the bust of The Sun King, (King Louis XIV) he joked to the king saying, "If I would have carved it a little bit more, it would have spoken." That's how alive the bust appeared. One only has to visit St. Peter's in Rome, to realize it is almost a Bernini museum, or the Galleria Borghese.

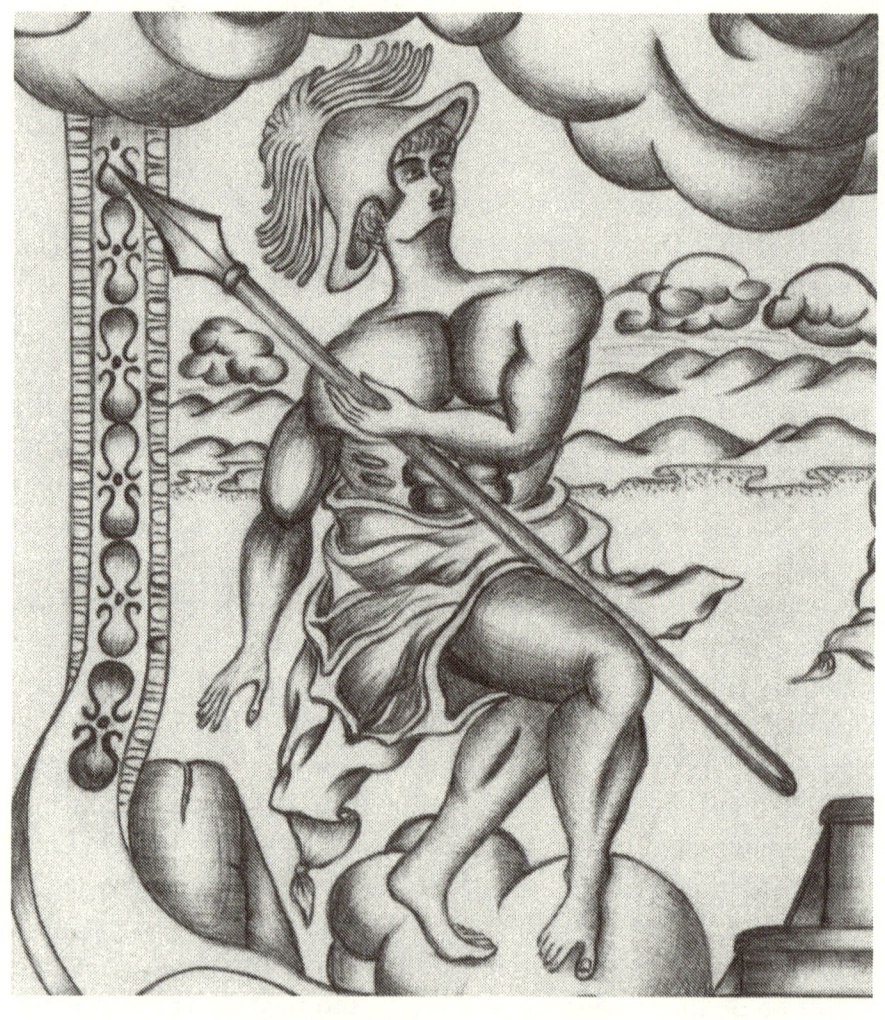

The conversion of Longinus

The life of Kind David has fascinated historians, writers and artists, and has been a major issue of debate as to how he accomplished his victories. Here the intention is to portray the virtue Justice *(Justitia)* as part of the heroic events that happened in David's life. David has just finished defeating the Philistine army after slaying Goliath the giant. Being a shepherd boy, at the end of the day he goes back to the wilderness to gather his father's flock. On his way he encounters a lion which he battles to its death with his bare hands. There is no record that indicates that this actual event happened, but there are accounts that David battled lions and bears that attacked his father's flock. I have improvised and added all these heroic events into one scene.

This scene is divided into three realms. The earthly realm, with David, and Justice, the intermediate realm, and the celestial realm. In the intermediate realm there are four angels carrying instruments that led David to the throne. On the far right is an angel carrying a *harp*, above it is an angel carrying a shepherd's *staff*, in the middle we see an angel carrying a leather *sling*, and to the far left is an angel with a smooth *stone* in its right hand. The fifth instrument is the *sword* that Justice is carrying which David used to cut off the head of Goliath after hitting him with the stone from his sling. Those are the five instruments that led David to the throne each of which has a symbolic meaning to it.

In the celestial realm is the Holy Trinity and angelic hosts. Heaven splits open in awe to marvel and cheer this triumphant young warrior. Based on the chronicles of his life, David's faith in God's ability to give him victory in his battles is what sustained him.

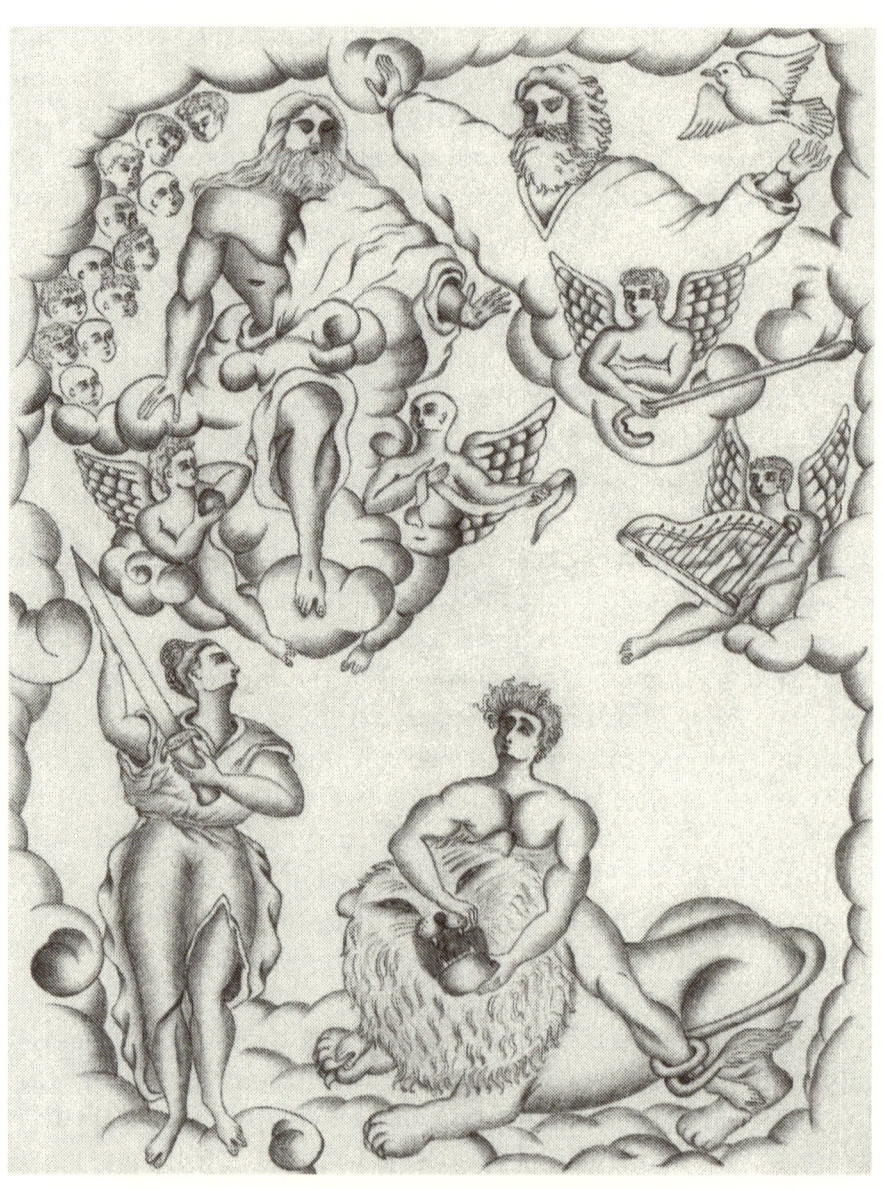

Justice–The Triumph Of David

Let us take a look at each of the five instruments David used. This detailed rendering of Justice, shows her standing with a classical *contrapposto* pose while holding a *sword*. When David struck Goliath with a rock, the giant fell and was unconscious. David then ran toward him and pulled out Goliath's own sword from its sheath, and used it to cut off his head. Goliath was the greatest Philistine warrior of his day and was feared by all. He was known for taunting and intimidating those who tried to stand up against him.

Being the defiant warrior that he was, David was the only one with courage enough to challenge Goliath. David himself had been practicing in the wilderness and had perfected the art of using a sling and stone to devastate the enemy. He used it against fully-grown bears and lions, so when he challenged Goliath, he knew that Goliath was too big a target for him to miss. David then took one of the five stones out the bag he was carrying, slipped it into the sling, and took a shot. The force within the stone sent Goliath tumbling down, and Goliath's head was cut off with the very weapon he intended to use against David. It was at that moment that Justice was served. The reason why David carried five stones with him was because the Philistines normally had five generals leading their armies. Goliath was the leader of them all. David was simply preparing for any possible contingencies. So the sword represents David's fame as a warrior.

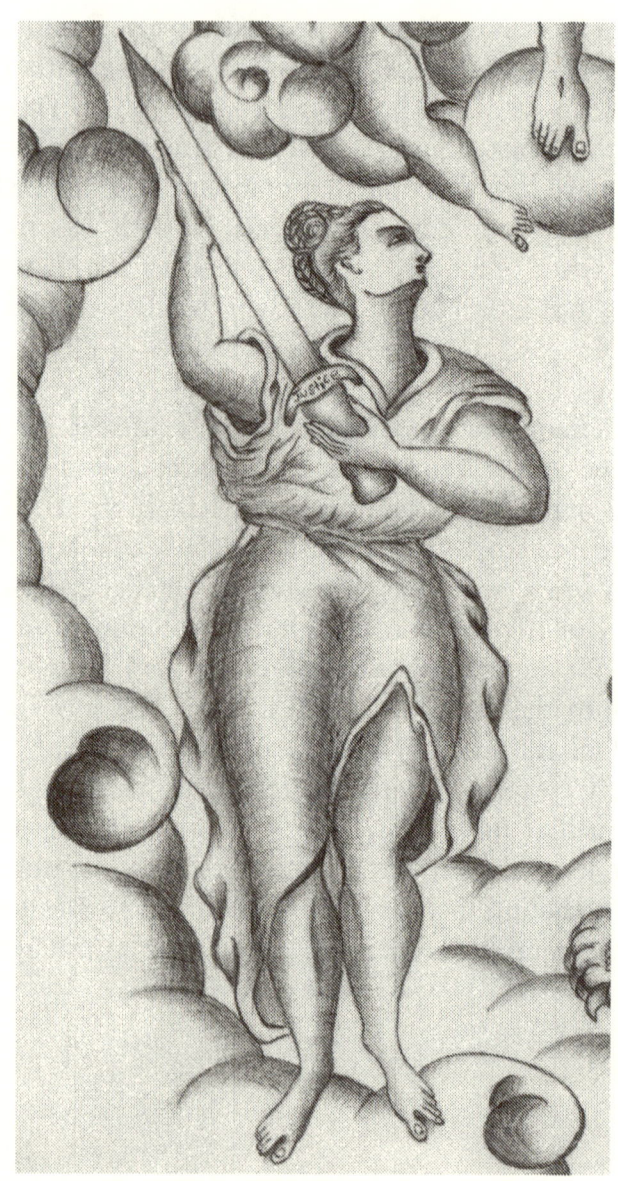

Detail Of Justice

The second instrument is the *sling*, and is being carried by the angel to the right. The sling represents David's victory to the throne after slaying the giant. This weapon was used by David and his men throughout their battles, even after he became king. It is chronicled in scripture that David's best soldiers were so well trained by him, they could use a sling with the left hand as well as they could with the right hand. His men were also well known for their courage and loyalty to David. One day three of his men went to a rock where David was staying, while a band of Philistines was camping in a nearby valley. David got homesick and said, "How I wish someone would bring me a drink of water from the well by the gate in Bethlehem!" At this time the Philistines had occupied Bethlehem. These three of David's men forced their way through the Philistine camp, drew some water out of the well, and brought it back to David. David refused to drink it, because he was so touched by the way they had risked their lives for his sake. He instead poured it as an offering to the Lord.

The third instrument is the *stone* that's being held by the angel on the left. The rock represents David's rock-solid faith in God's ability to make him victorious.

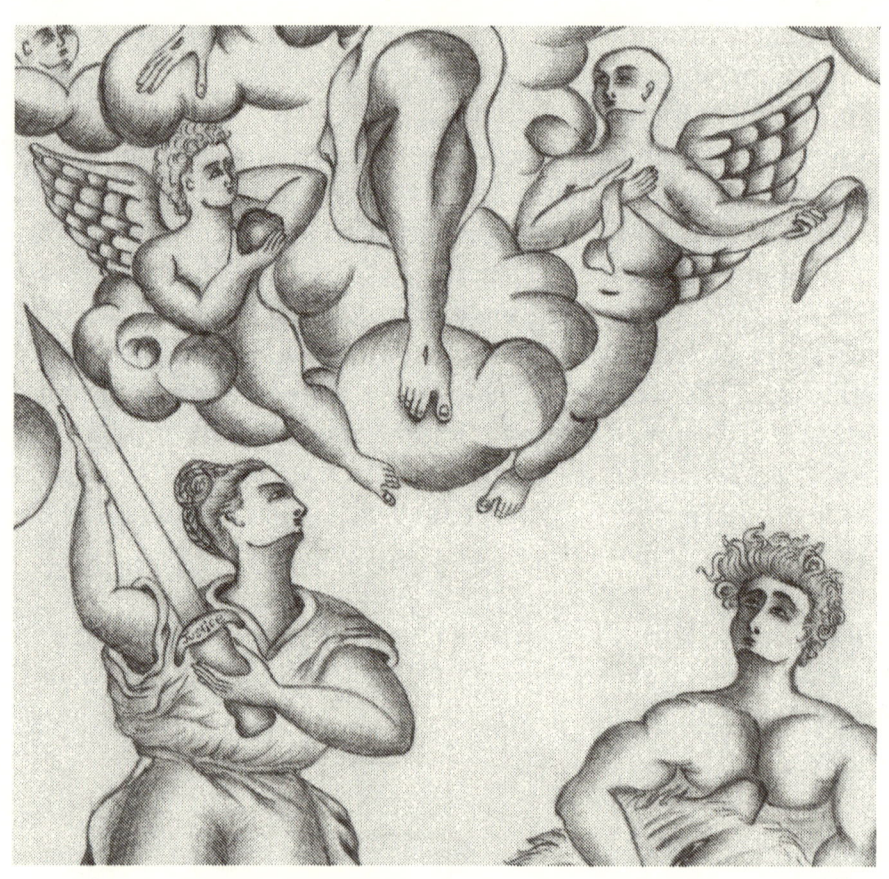

Detail of the angels with sling and stone

The fourth instrument is the *staff*. The staff represents his skill as a shepherd. He had spent most of his years as a youth in the wilderness tending to his father's sheep. He used the staff to guide the flock and to defend them against wild animals. On the day David defeated Goliath, he was carrying his staff with him. Goliath started walking toward David and when he saw David's staff, he got angry and said, "What's that stick for? Do you think I am a dog?" He then started cursing David. At that point David too was filled with indignation and ran quickly toward Goliath and struck him with one of the five smooth stones that broke his skull. Goliath dropped to his knees and was beheaded.

Lastly, the fifth instrument is the *harp*. Not only was David a warrior, he was also a worshipper who composed thousands of songs. He played his harp in the wilderness when he was bored, and was frequently invited to the palace to play it for king Saul. You see king Saul was vexed by an evil spirit, but every time David played beautiful music with his harp, the evil spirit would leave king Saul and the king would have peace of mind. It was David's skill as a musician that created the frequent royal invitations. The harp therefore represents David's skill as a musician and worshipper.

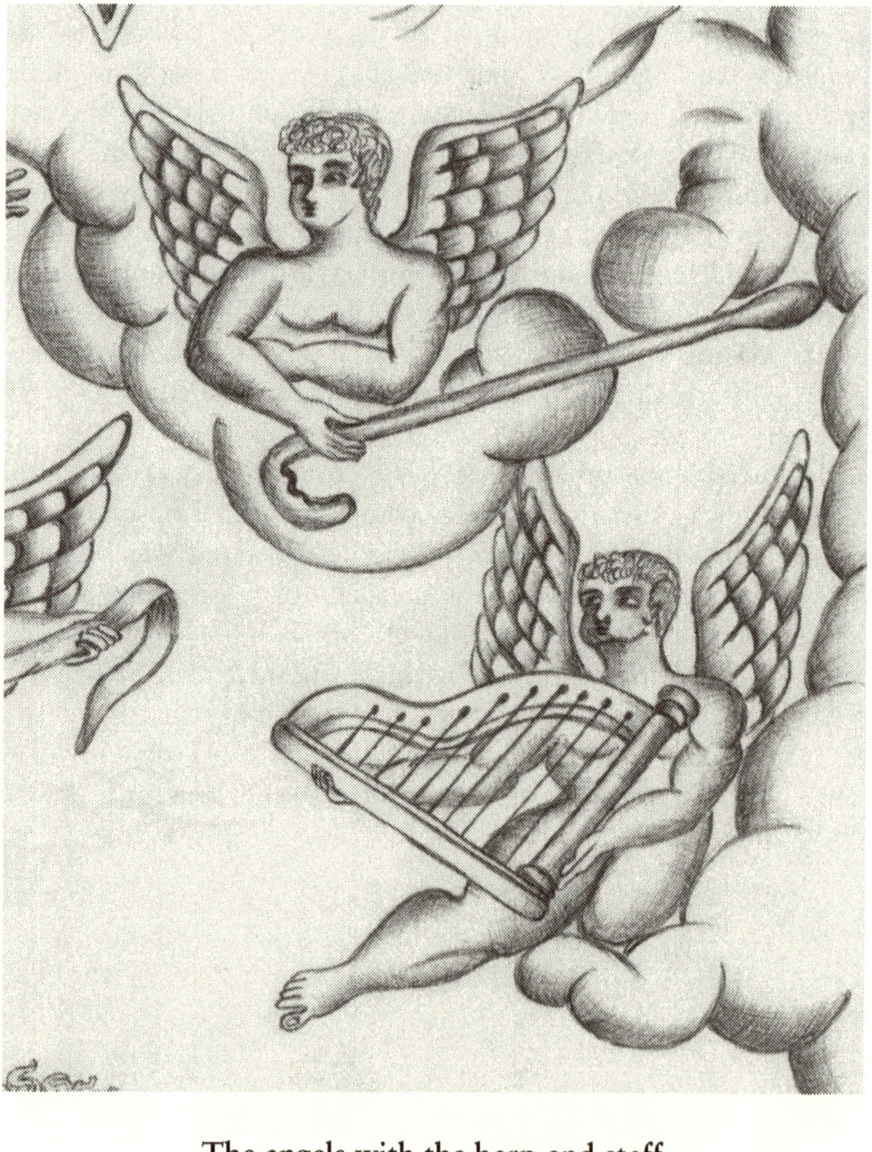

The angels with the harp and staff

Confronting an adult African lion (*Panthera Leo*) and battling it with one's bare hands requires a lot of strength and bravery. David had done so on many occasions. When a bear or lion carried off a lamb, David would attack it, and rescue the lamb. If either the bear or lion turned against David, he would grab it by the throat and beat it to death. Before anyone can grab a lion by the throat, you have to be in close proximity and place yourself in a position that doesn't leave you vulnerable. Here, I use creative imagination to place David in a strategic stance. He steps on the lion's hind leg and front paw to prevent it from moving back or forth, and also to protect himself from the lion's dangerous claws. If you take a closer look, David has also placed his weight on the lion's back, that way the lion stays put. In case the lion tries to stand up, David uses his weight to keep the lion down by sitting on it. Now that he is in a secure stance, David uses his might to open the lion's mouth in order for the lamb to be released. He eventually dislocates the lower and upper jaws, for his own protection. With both jaws dislocated, David grabs the lion from behind by its windpipe and suffocates it to a state of unconsciousness. He then consummates the lion's demise by beating it to death between the eyes using his shepherd's staff.

David's bravery and defiance were contagious. A story is told of one of David's loyal men by the name of Benaiah who went down into a pit on a snowy day, and killed a lion. It is no wonder the life of David still intrigues many. David is shown gazing toward heaven, because that's where he gets his supernatural strength.

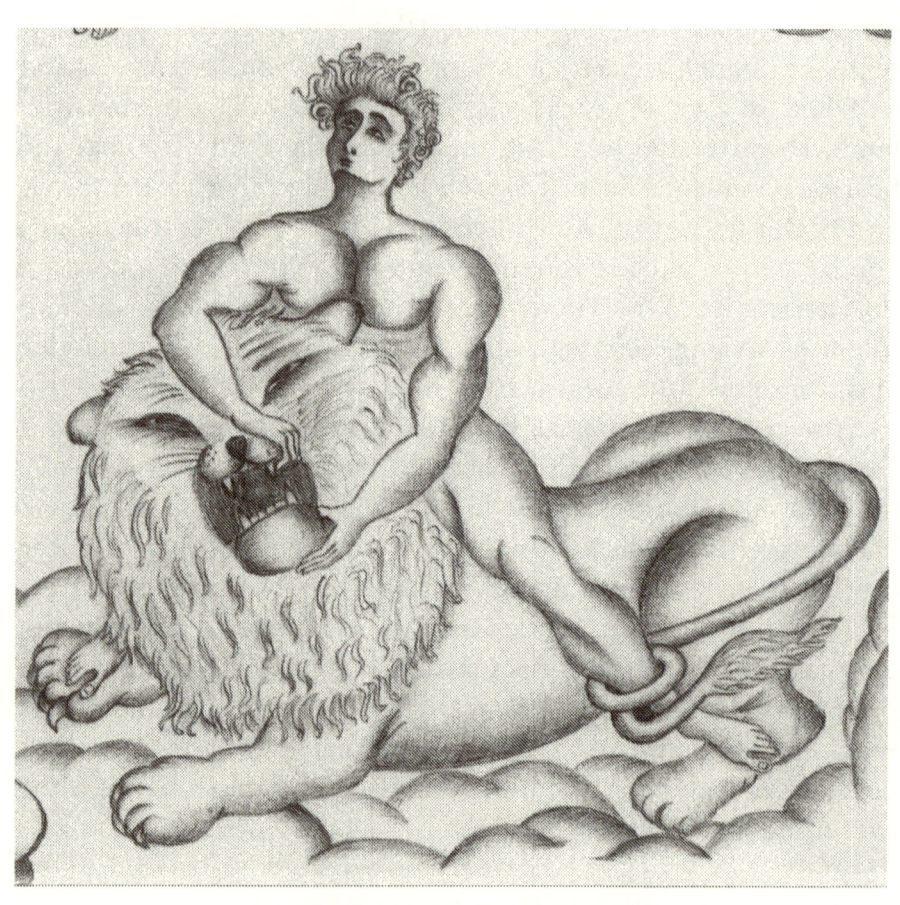

The Triumph Of David

While David was confronting his adversaries, heaven was watching. God the Father is seen with the Holy Spirit in the celestial realm, stretching the skies open to witness David in action. God the Son is shown seated at the right side of God the Father. To the right of Christ are twelve little angels. The number twelve means *rulership*, and this is the next phase of David's life. Beneath the Holy Trinity are four more angels (*cherubim*), in the intermediate realm.

Not only do the cherubim serve the purpose of carrying the instruments David used, they also represent the four element (*speculum naturale*) which are: water, wind, earth, and fire.

Cherubim are the second highest rank of angels in the celestial hierarchy. The highest in the celestial order are seraphim. Cherubs and seraphim are the closest to God and are always in His presence. The celestial hierarchy, beginning with the highest ranking, is in the following nine orders: seraphim, cherubim, thrones, dominions, virtues, powers, principalities, archangels, and angels, which are the lowest in rank.

Christ is shown stretching out His hand to impart upon David blessings that will make him victorious in all his battles.

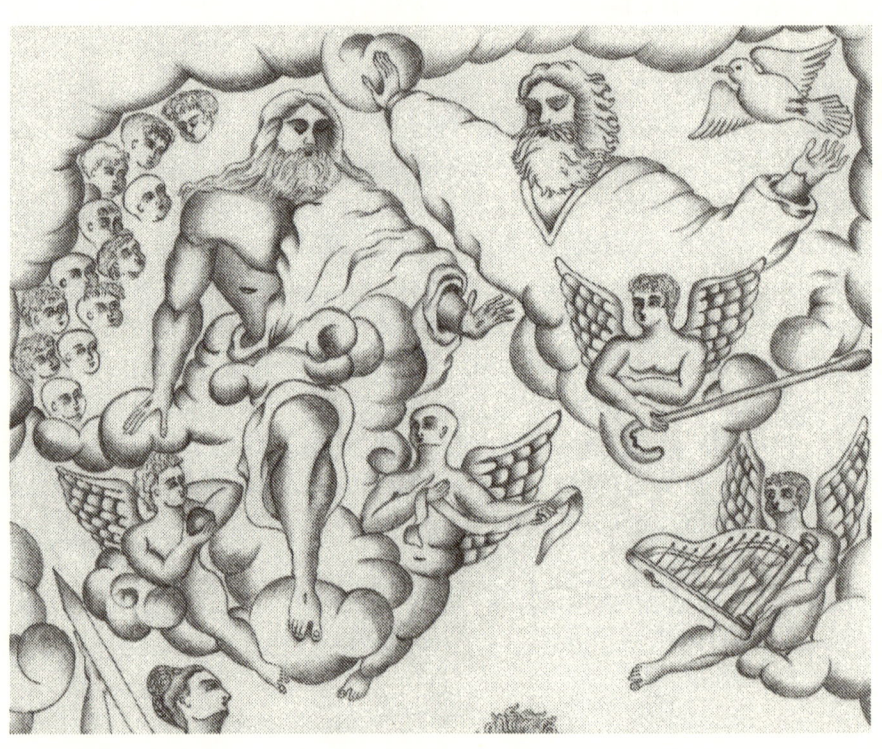

The Trinity In Glory

In an earlier chapter, I mentioned that I would briefly talk about the seven liberal arts (*artes liberales*). They are called the seven liberal arts because their purpose is to train the free man. The liberal arts are divided into two distinctive groups. The first group is also referred to as *language studies*. These are: Grammar (Science of language), Oratory (Science of rhetoric), and Dialectic (Science of logic). The next group includes Arithmetic, Music, Geometry and Astronomy. These disciplines are referred to as *Mathematic studies*. Grammar tops the list because it is considered to be the greatest of all the liberal arts. Grammar has the power to create or destroy. Grammar is also the backbone of all literature and language. However, each of the liberal arts is equally important and they all serve each other. The order in which the liberal arts are arranged has been a great cause of debate, from ancient Greek philosophers to High Renaissance scholars. I try not to let myself get too perturbed by any philosophical speculation, so I will leave the seven liberal arts in the order in which they are arranged.

I have included only two of the seven liberal arts, because the main purpose of this book is to celebrate the virtues. In this drawing we see Grammar reaching out to Music. The love story between Grammar and Music unfolds when Grammar uses literature to entice Music, who reciprocates with the musical instrument that she is carrying. This romantic exchange is captured in the following verses.

Grammar: *There is ballad I sing, that I wrote for you*
             The words you hear, will forever be true
             From heart to heart, this is yours from me
             Accept it in your life, I ask of thee.

Music:　　My precious one, my dearest friend
The sweetest thoughts, to you I send
When you search my heart, you will always find
Special musical notes, that only love can bind.

Faith, Hope, and Divine Love or Charity, were the three other virtues that were later on introduced by Gregory The Great to make up the seven virtues. All three virtues are in harmony with each other. Divine Love (*Caritas*) is undeniably the greatest and most beautiful of all the virtues combined, that's why she sits aloft the rest of them. The eagle serves as a double compliment to the entire composition. The soaring wings represent Father Time, since of course every virtue is ultimately revealed by time. The eagle itself celebrates the words of the prophet Isaiah who wrote, "…They will rise upon wings like eagles."

Charity is seen comforting the weary Faith with tenderness, and is also affirming Hope with a loving gaze of meekness and compassion. The idea of the virtues riding on an eagle was drawn from tales that were told in the past about eagles snatching away infants that were unsupervised. Whether fact or fiction, the larger eagles have the capability of doing just that. One type of eagle that comes to mind is the largest of the African eagles, the grandiose Martial Eagle (*Hieraaetus bellicosus*). It can catch a mammal as large as a baboon or even a young impala. I use the eagle in this drawing for allegorical purposes and to add richness to my work. If you look back to the preceding chapters, you'll notice that I have used animals that we admire for their speed, strength and nobility. We've seen the horse, lion, and now the eagle. This was intentional on my behalf because these are the most popular creatures, and throughout the centuries, they've been used on emblems, coat of arms, and even the early Egyptians carved them on tablets and inside their tombs, for the purpose of story telling.

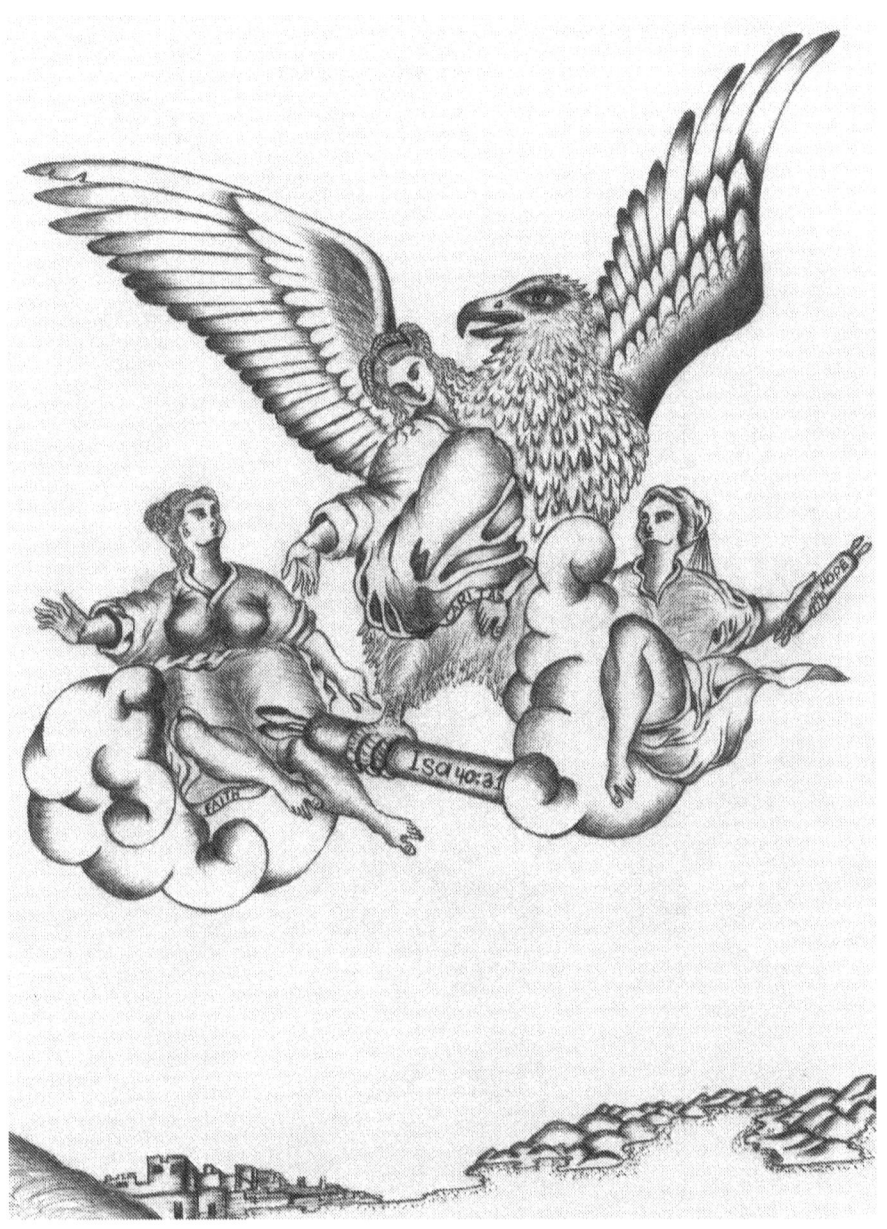

Faith, Hope, and Love

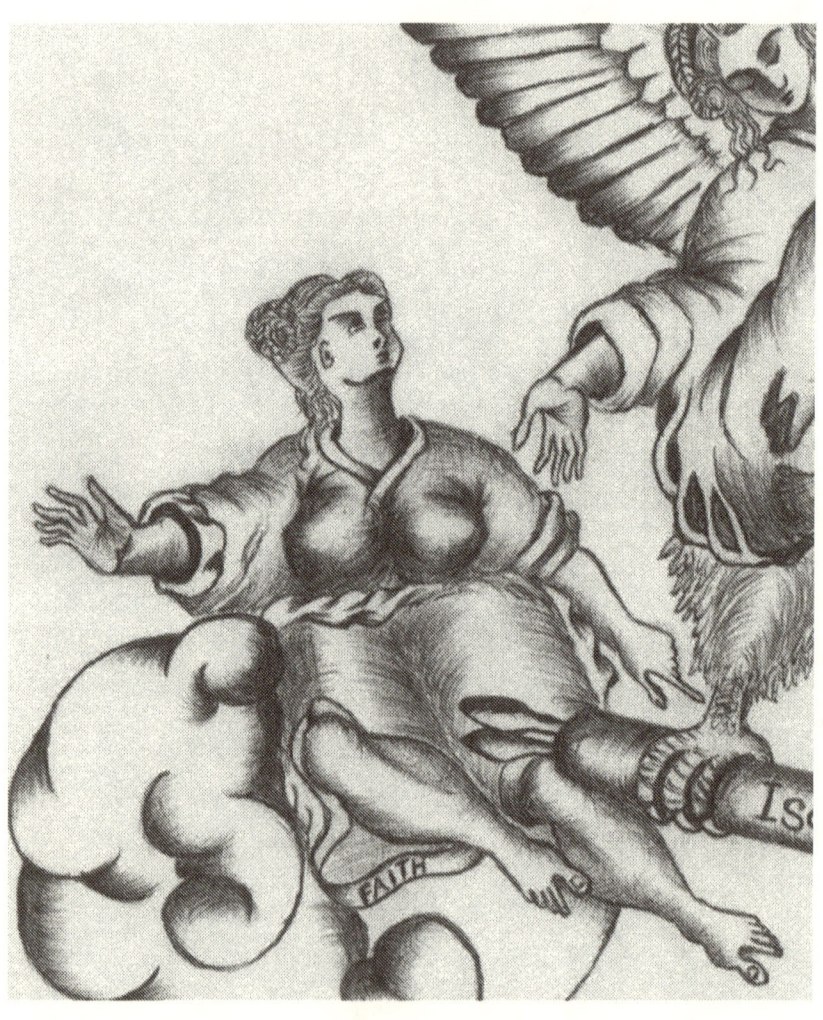

Detail Of Faith

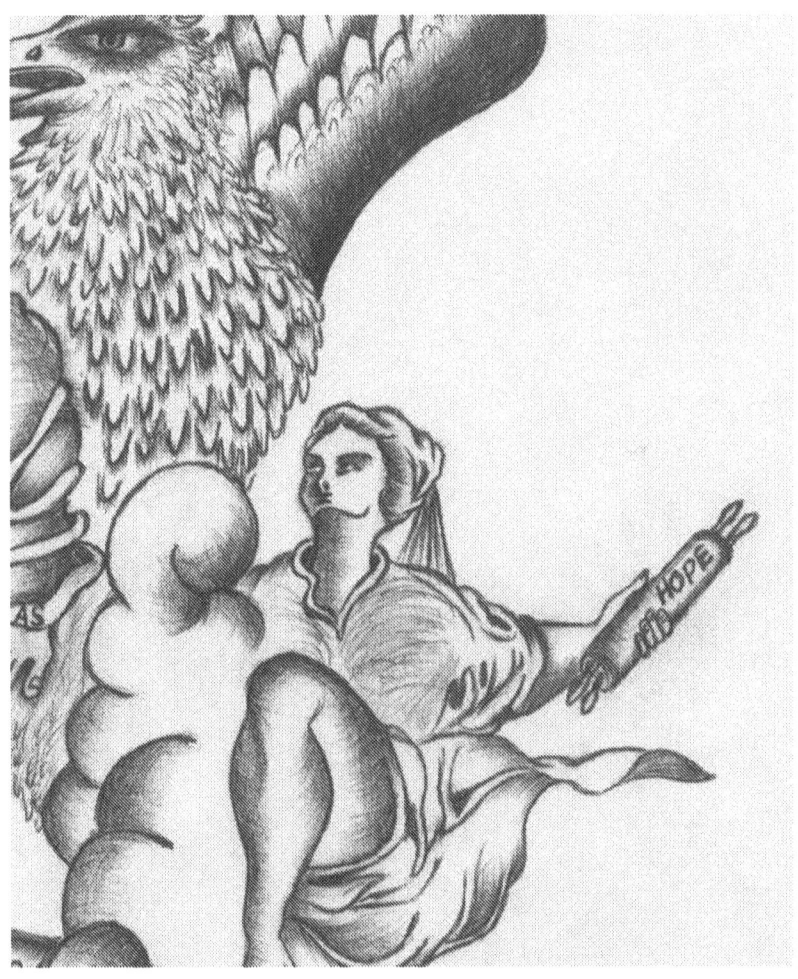

Detail Of Hope

PART II

The Creation Of The Virtues

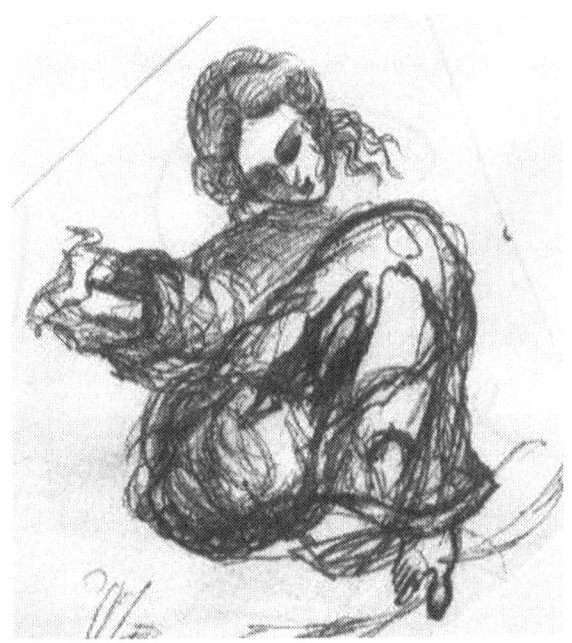

In this section, you will see the step-by-step process I apply to create the virtues and the rest of my artwork. Before I create the final rendition of any drawing, I create a series of rough sketches in preparation for the final rendering. These sketches will provide you with some insight on what goes on within my mind, while I'm creating my work.

The detail of the final drawings shows how important it is to pay attention to the face, the gestures, and the pose of a figure within a composition. As I mentioned earlier, in order to prepare myself for this undertaking, I studied how the Greeks and Romans created their work. The Greeks drew inspiration from Egyptian works, and then refined the arts. While most of the Egyptian drawings were in profile, the Greeks drew and sculpted in relief and perspective. It took the Greeks only two hundred years to develop a culture that dominated all areas of the arts. They were masters of theater, drama, poetry, sculpture and the rest of the liberal arts. The Romans then took what they had learned from the Greeks to a higher level, and produced harmonious masterpieces. The greatest of the Renaissance painters, Raphael, spent a considerable amount of time excavating and studying ancient artistic works. You can tell the influence classical antiquity had on Raphael by his Madonnas. He was able to eclipse his contemporaries because he could draw female figures, just as well as he could the male nude (*Kouros*).

When the mannerists came along, led by Caravaggio and Carracci, art flourished like never before. They were able to integrate Greek mythology into their work in order to affect viewers like no other group of artists had. Mannerism continued until the late sixteenth and early seventeenth century, thereafter was the rise of the Baroque artists namely: Bernini, Borromini, and Pietro da Cortona. Their influence was so contagious, it helped spread their style throughout Europe, and it was truly a triumph of the arts. The public and private patrons who supported these artists, are chiefly responsible for the flourishing of the arts during the counter-reformation.

These patrons had an appreciation for the arts, and felt it was their earthly duty to seek those who were gifted in the arts and give them a platform to share their work with the rest of the world. As centuries went by, art became less and less appreciated, and artists spent less time developing their craft. With modern technology, one doesn't even have to know how to draw to create a piece, so there is less emphasis on learning the basics, as opposed to the time when the ancient masters created true art.

In **The Virtues Unveiled,** I go back to the basics and draw everything with my very own hand. The toughest part for me in creating my work is choosing the right kind of pen to use. Sometimes a pen might have an irregular flow of ink, which causes some of the lines to appear thicker than others. The perfect pen is one that has an even flow of ink that produces fine lines. It is hard to know which pen will suit my needs sometimes I'm just fortunate to find the right one.

Before I create my work, I have absolutely no idea what I'm going to draw, until the pen hits the paper. After creating a series of sketches, I select one that I feel is suitable, and start building a theme from there.

Since I'm my worst critic, the first final rendition usually doesn't make it, because after about two weeks when I look at it again, I may not feel it is worthy of public display, so I end up re-doing the whole piece.

The main purpose of the work in this book is to celebrate the arts in the 21st century. The work herein, is meant to appeal not only to the intellect, but also to the emotions of the viewer. In other words, I consider my art to be an art of persuasion. Some of the subjects in this book were briefly explored, however, in my next project, I expect to take an in-depth look at them.

Even though I placed a lot of emphasis on studying the ancients, I was careful to maintain my individualism, which allowed me to create work that is totally different and cannot be associated with being influenced by any one particular artist. Once you've drawn inspiration from someone else, it's important to blaze your own trail, with artistic compositions that are uniquely yours.

The Virtues Unveiled was initially called The Celebration Of The Virtues, but I thought that was a very long title for a book. It would work for something like a musical or a theatrical piece, but I felt for a book, I needed something shorter, that's when I came up with **The Virtues Unveiled.**

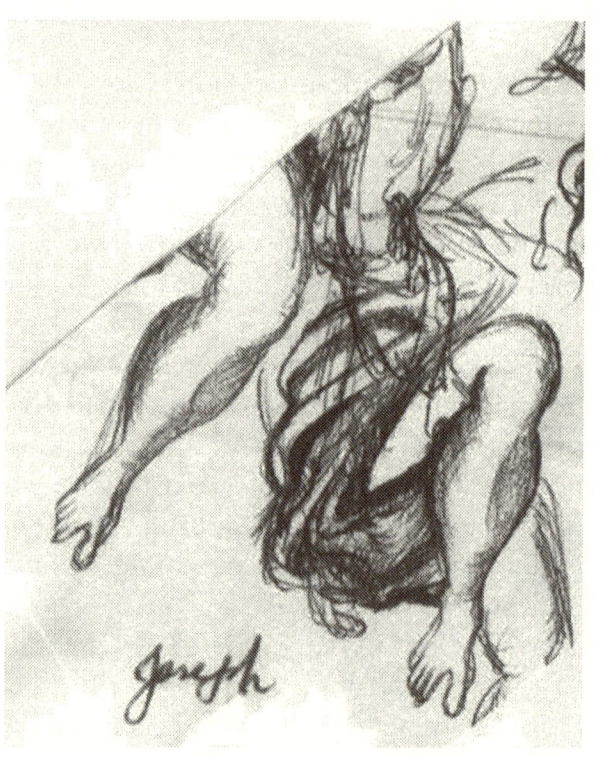

Preparatory study of Divine Love

In this initial rough sketch, I start out by drawing Charity's undraped lower body. The pose allows me to sit her on the eagle that will be carrying her.

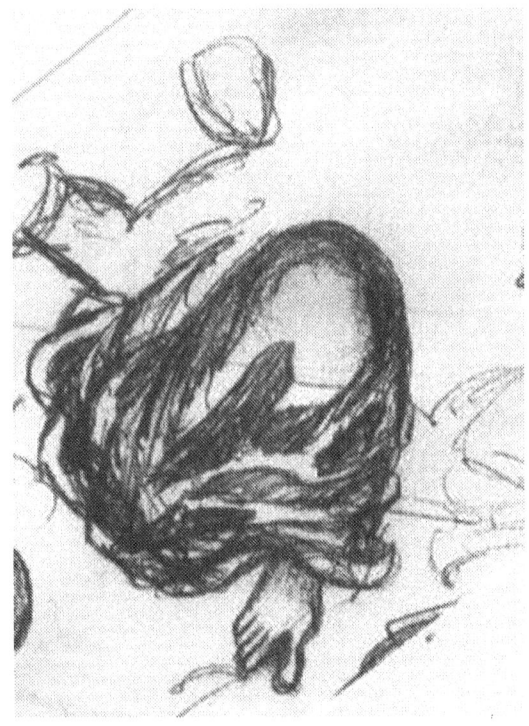

Sketch two

In this second sketch, I then proceed to drape Divine Love's entire body.

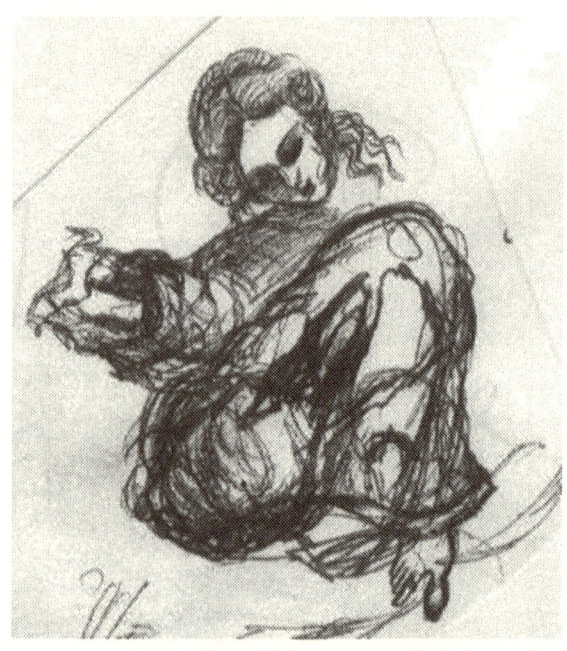

Sketch three

In this third sketch I concentrate on her facial features, giving her the aura of love, compassion, and tenderness, in all the manner-isms that she exudes.

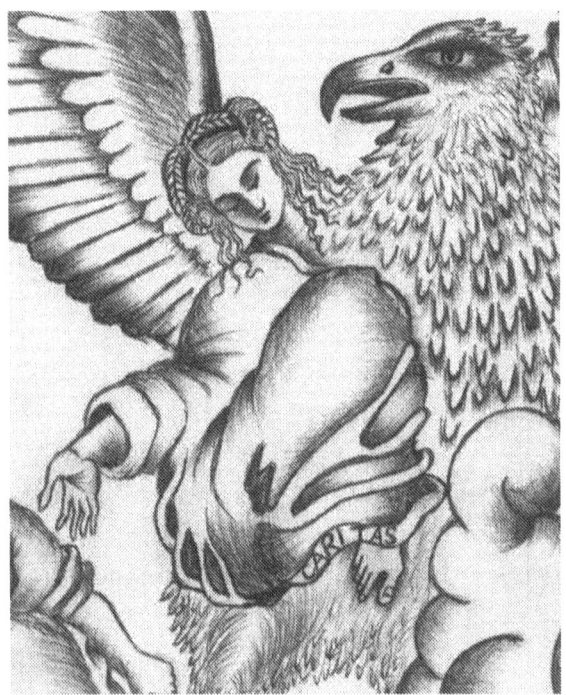

Detail of Divine Love in all her feminine glory.

In this final rendition, I present Divine Love to the viewer, for who she really is. Fully draped, and her hair styled in braids, she extends her compassion to both Faith and Hope, which is an indication that she not only possesses external beauty, which is evident, but she also has the noble internal beauty.

Study of David wrestling a lion

In this initial rough sketch, I am faced with a dilemma because I don't have a lion before me, so I improvise. I use myself as the model and draw an outline of my body-frame. As usual, I of course add a little more beef to the frame to give it a pumped-up look. Since David spent a lot of time laboring in the wilderness, it's obvious that he had a built frame, and had natural strength.

The tail of the lion wrapped around David's (my) left leg was inspired by an ancient Greek statue that I saw of Laocoön and his two sons being squeezed by serpents.

Whether or not a lion can wrap its tail around an object is of no great concern to me. My role as an artist is to be creative enough in all my artistic compositions, to create images that will deceive the human eye.

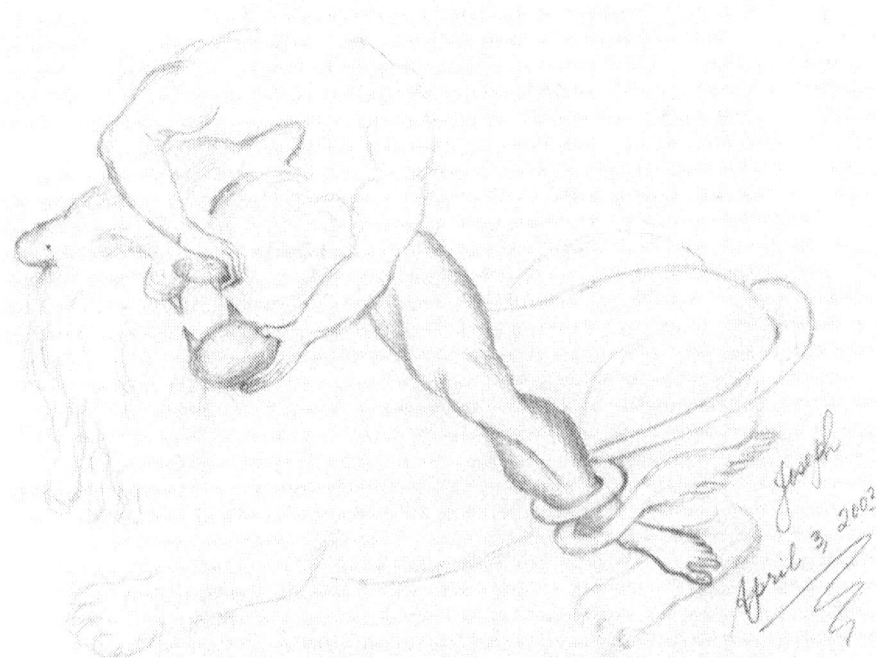

Initial rough sketch of David wrestling a lion.

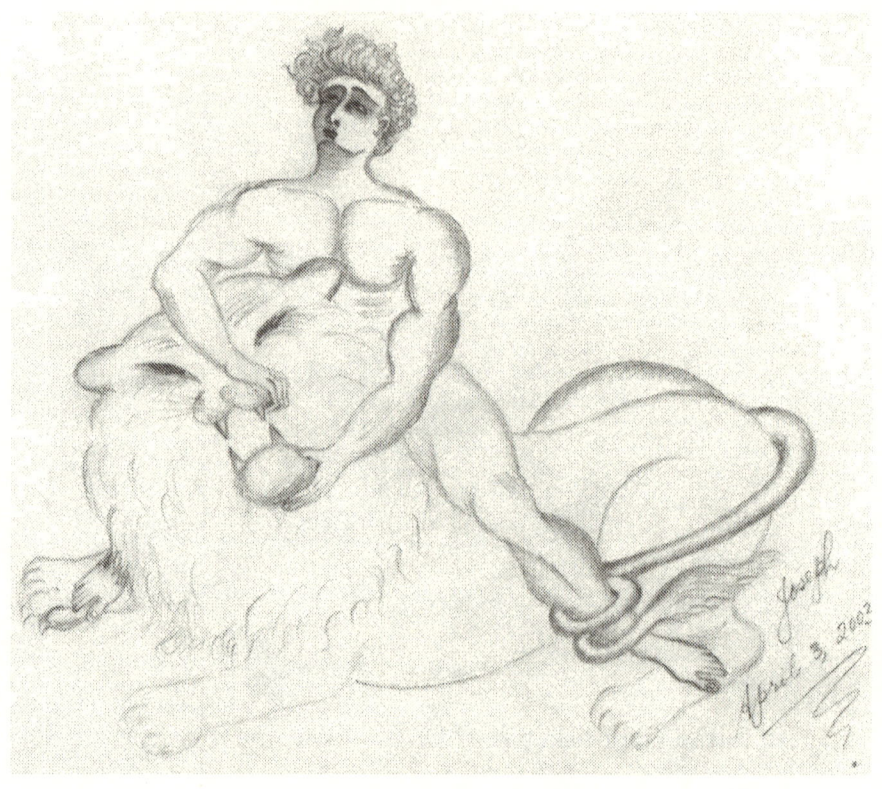

Study of David wrestling a lion

In this second rough sketch, David is battling the lion and his eyes are filled with passion. He had such passion about everything he did, whether it was during his battles, in his love life, or in his worship and writings.

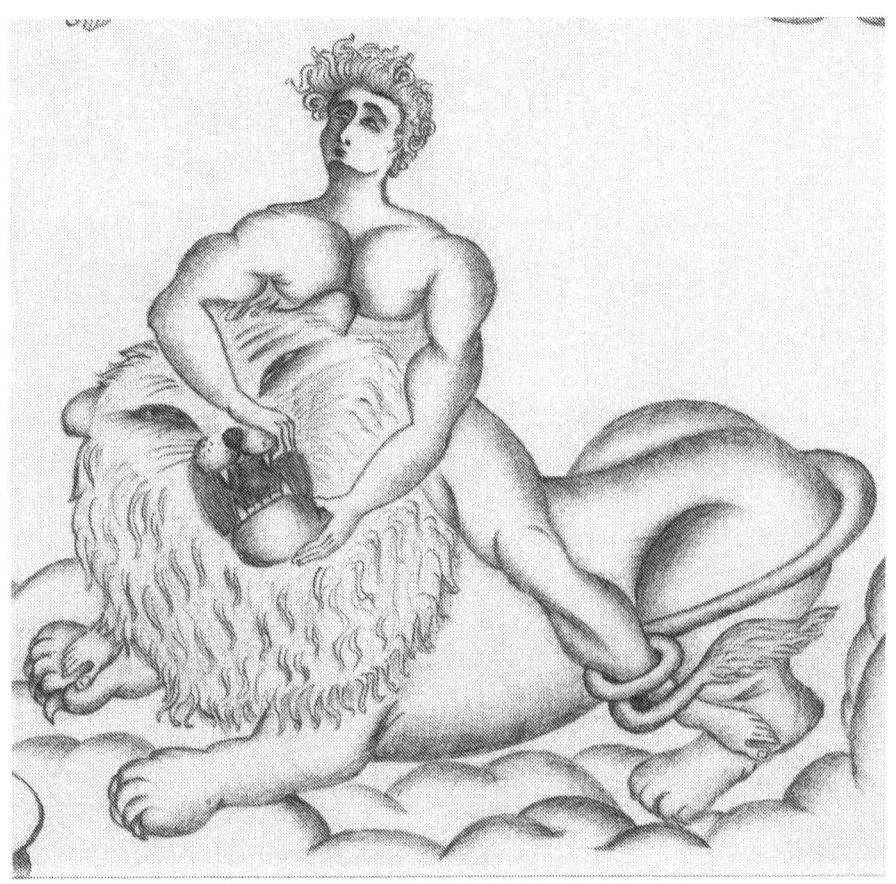

Detailed and final rendition–The Triumph Of David

The Creation of Truth.

Truth is one of my most favorite virtues and is closely related to Justice. I enjoyed working with Truth because I knew her true beauty would eventually be revealed by Time. In the following preparatory sketch, I quickly realize that she's the only virtue that rivals Charity in beauty. What sets Truth apart is she and time work hand in hand. The rest of the virtues can function independent of time.

The portrayal of Truth among the traditional virtues was popularized by Bernini, when his rival fellow artists tried to ruin his reputation and credibility. They told the new pope Innocent X that the bell tower Bernini had erected was threatening to collapse, and convinced the pope to order Bernini to remove it. The truth of the matter was, Bernini was the most gifted artist in the whole of Europe, and even when his reputation was on the line, he was able to redeem himself with time. In the end time indeed did reveal the genius of the Baroque master. More about Bernini can be found in his biographies by his very own son Domenico Bernini, also one by Filippo Baldinucci and Chantelou's diary.

There have been some suggest to me additional virtues in addition to the twelve included in this book, but for the moment, I'll focus on these twelve. At the end of this book, in the glossary section, I also talk about the seven vices, because you cannot have virtues without vices. I'm simply trying to create balance in my work. I did not put emphasis on Time because that's only here temporarily, and only exists with the universe. The virtues will live forever, and are beyond the confines of time. One can also interpret *The Triumph Of The Virtues—Youth and Age*, as a celebration of Truth and Time.

The third section of this book, which is the glossary, contains a summary and definitions of the highlights I talk about in **The Virtues Unveiled.**

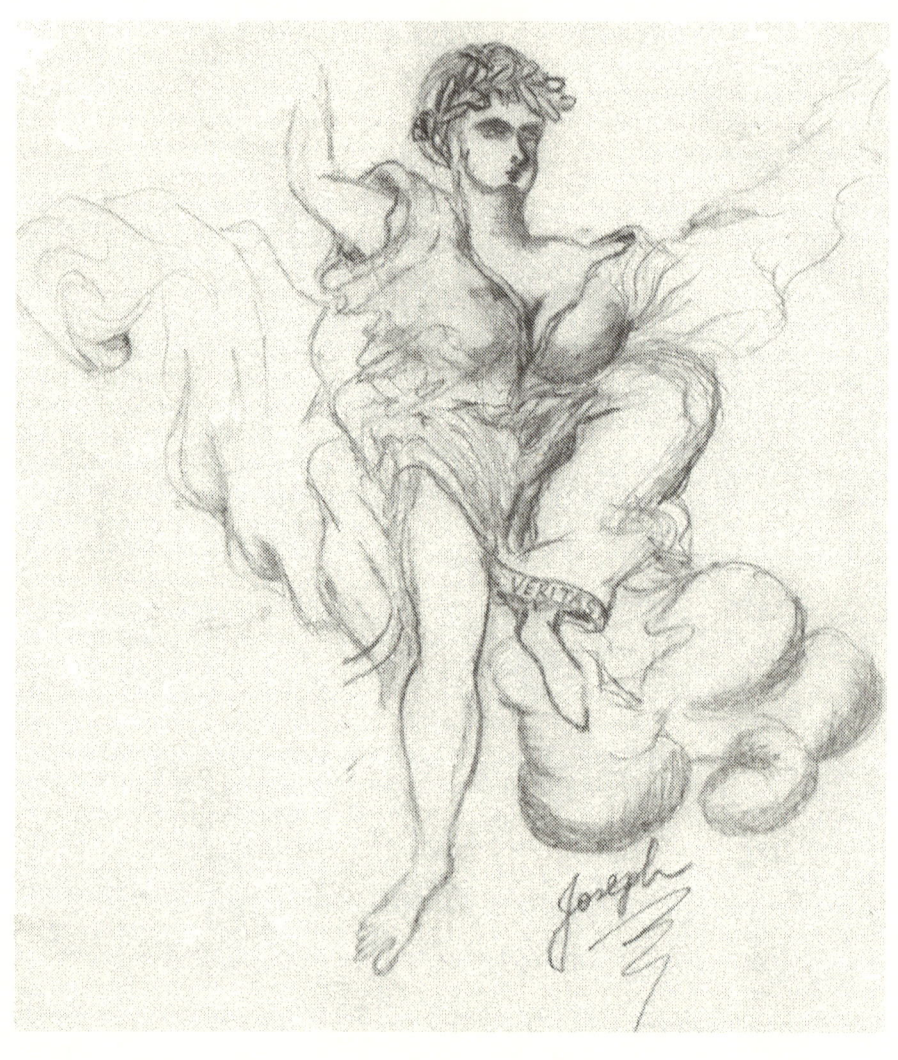

Study of Truth–rough sketch

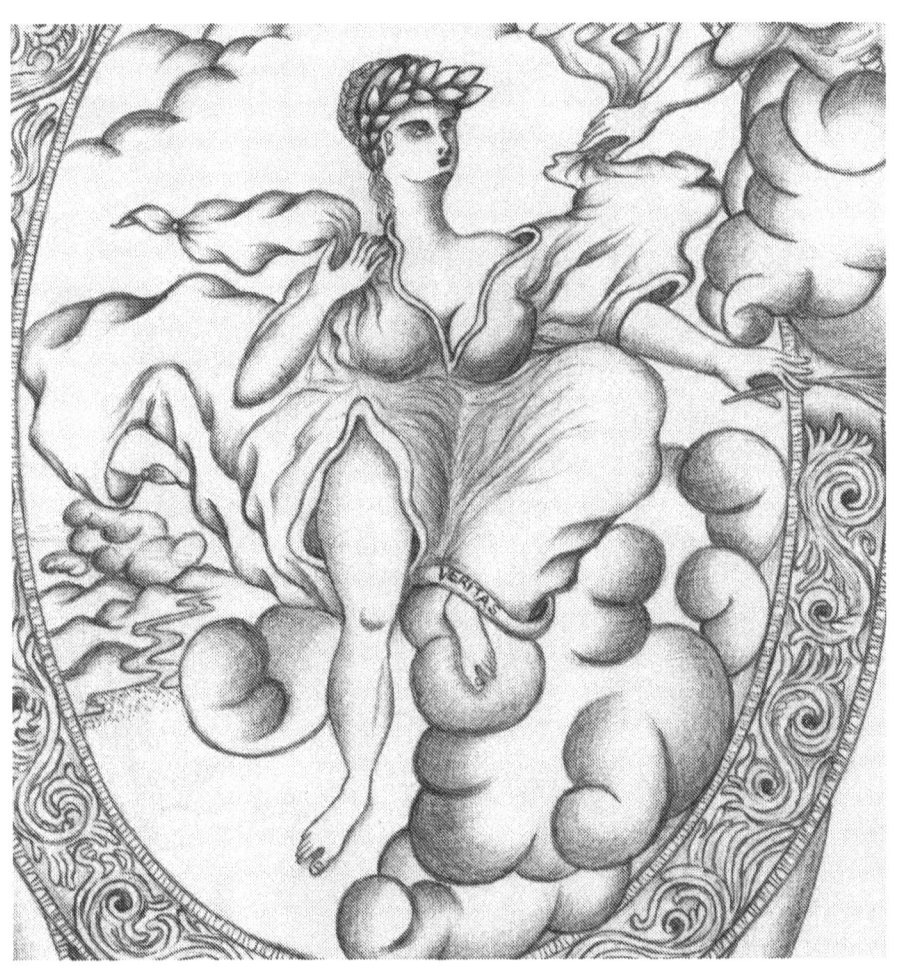

Detail of Truth

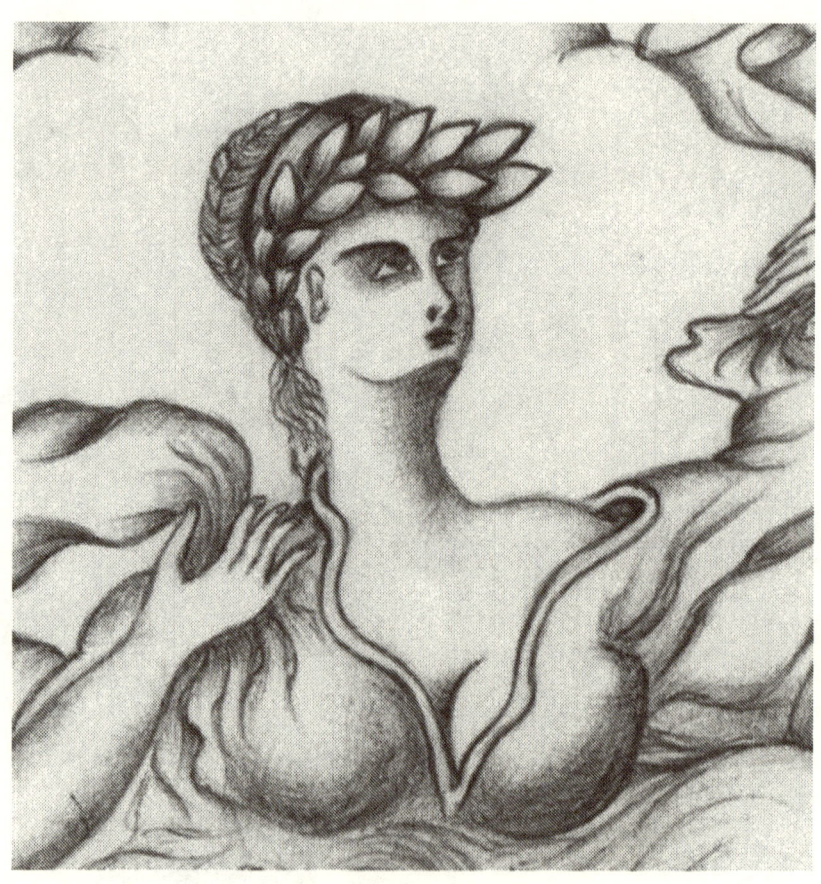

Head of Truth *(Veritas)*

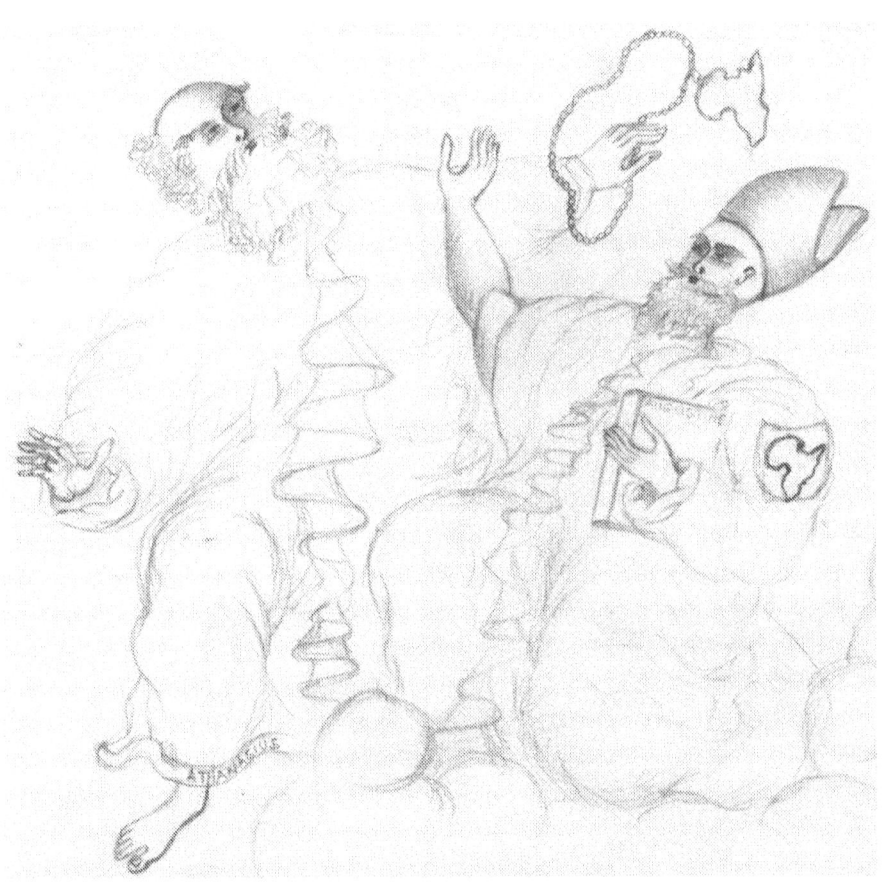

Study of St. Athanasius and St. Augustine–rough sketch

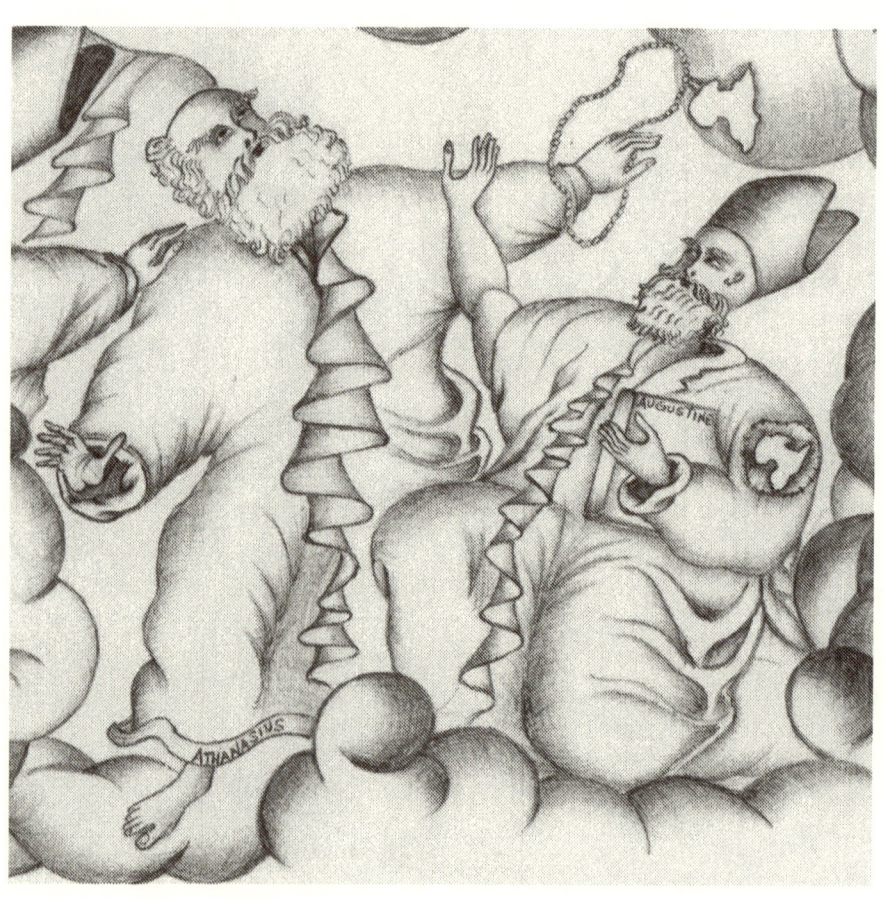

Detail of Athanasius and Augustine–final rendition.

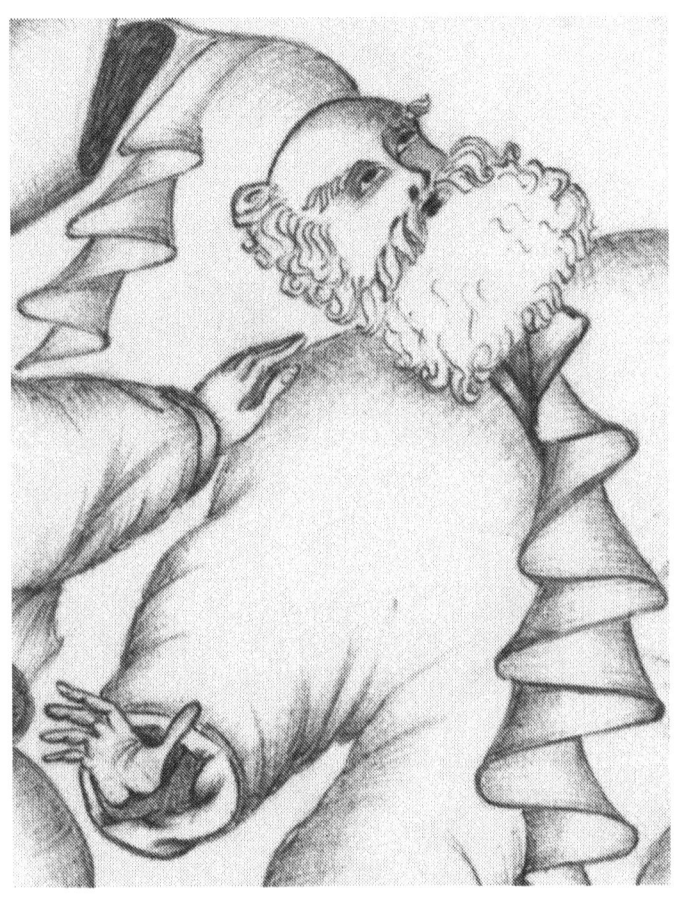

Head of Athanasius

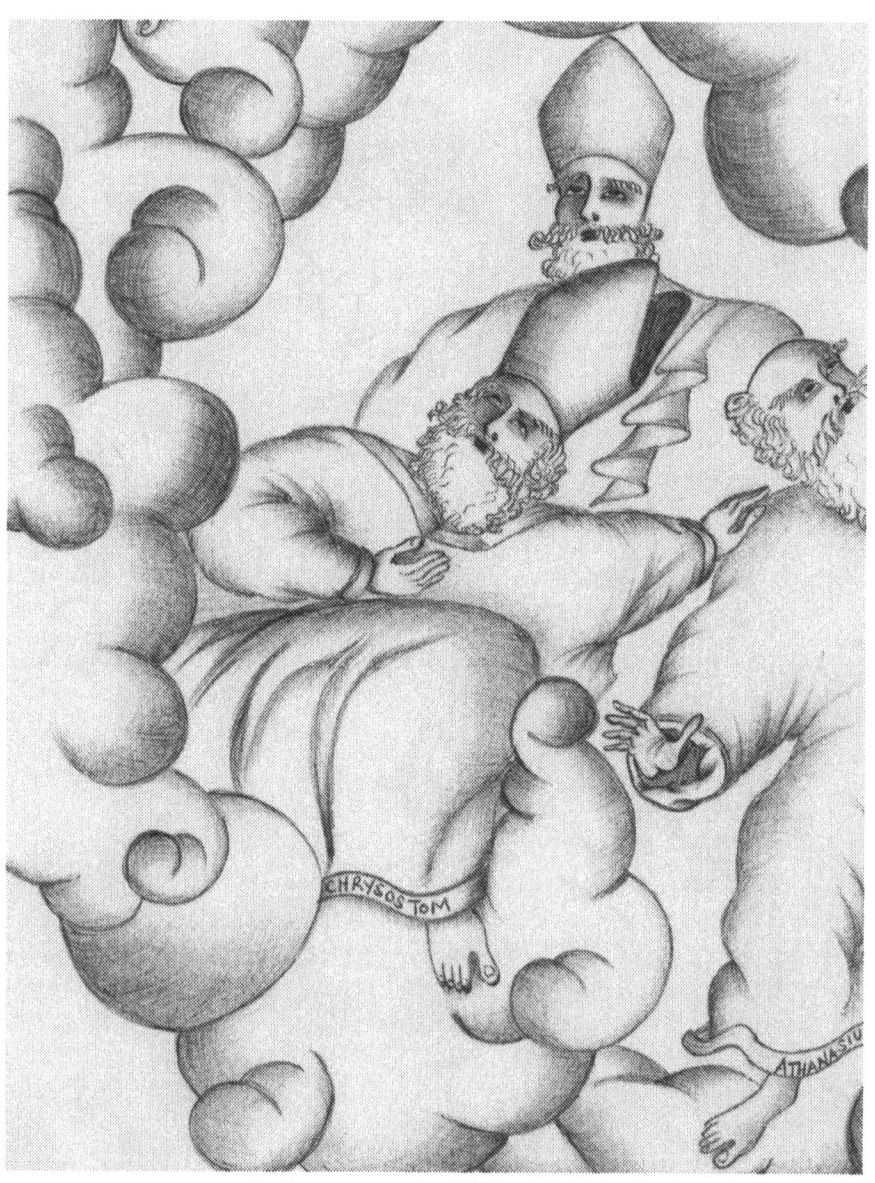

Detail of St. John Chrysostom and St. Ambrose

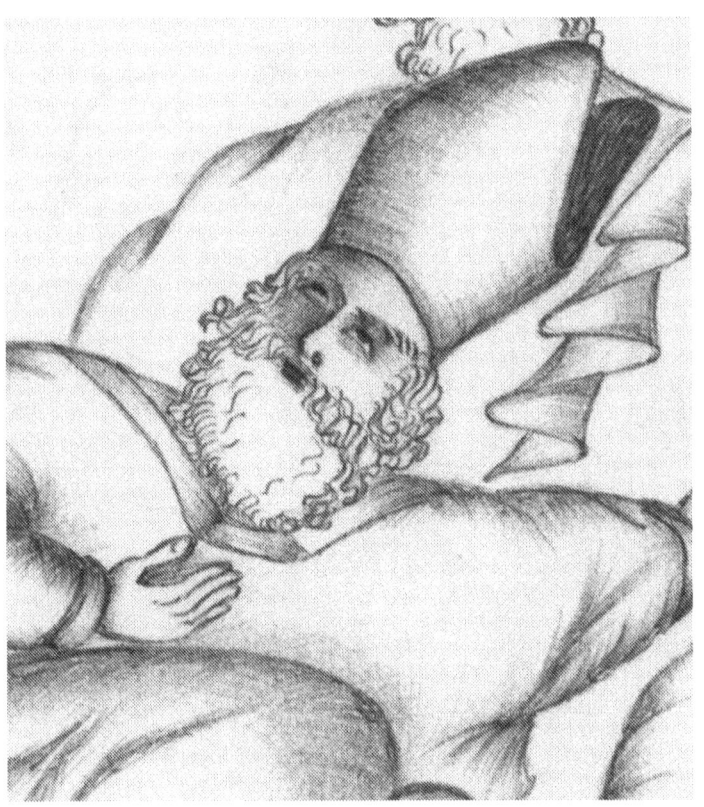

Head of John-Chrysostom

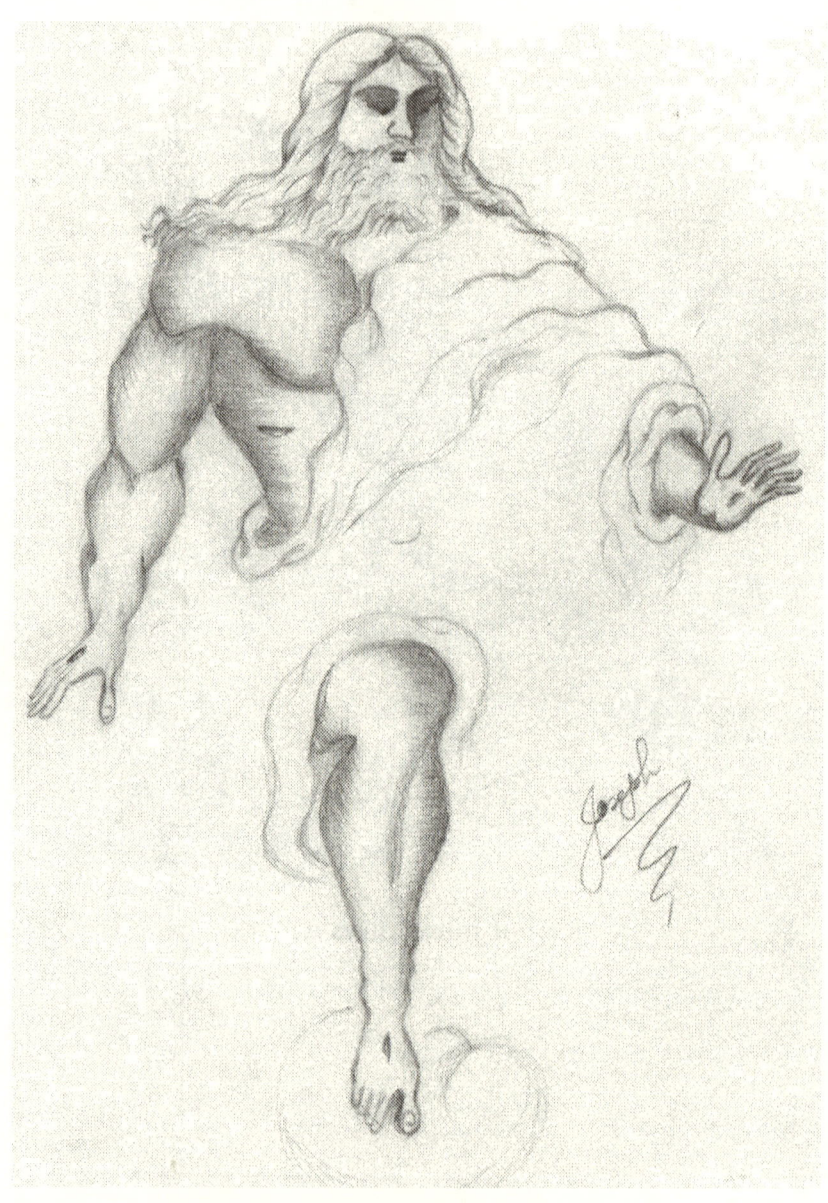

Study of Christ–preparatory sketch

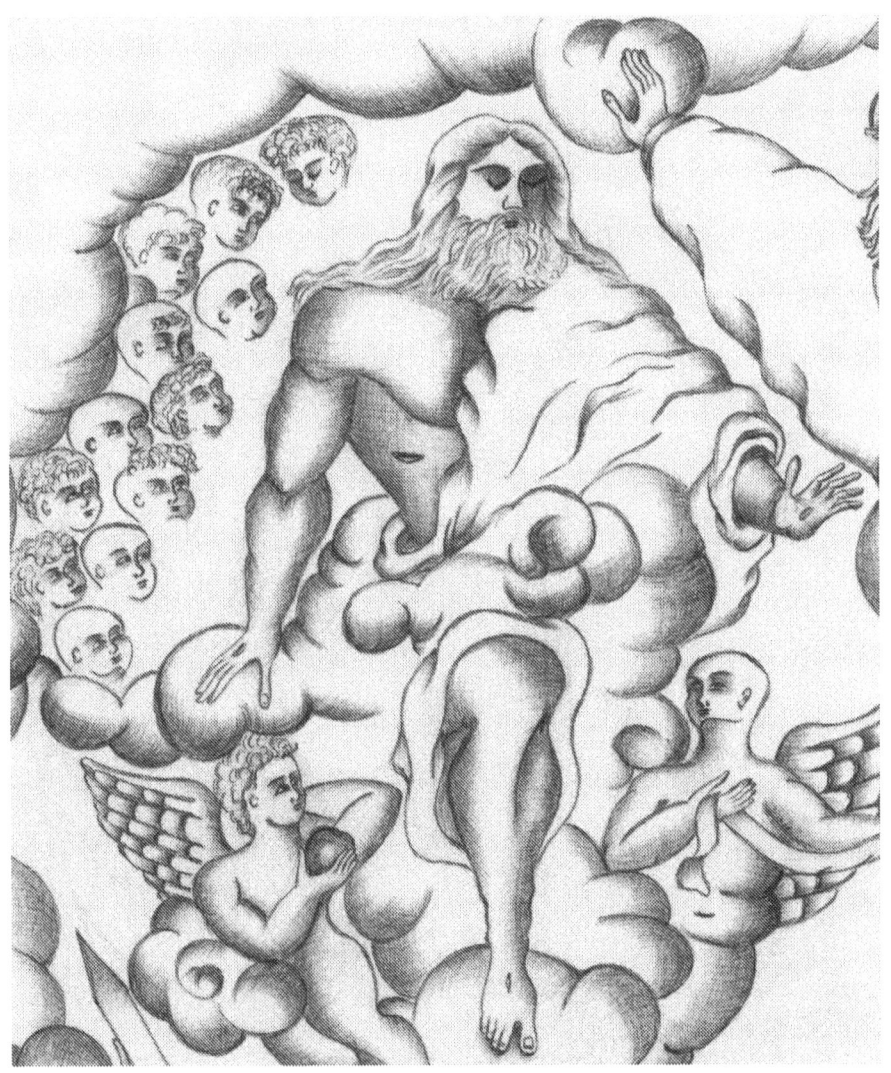

Detail of Christ

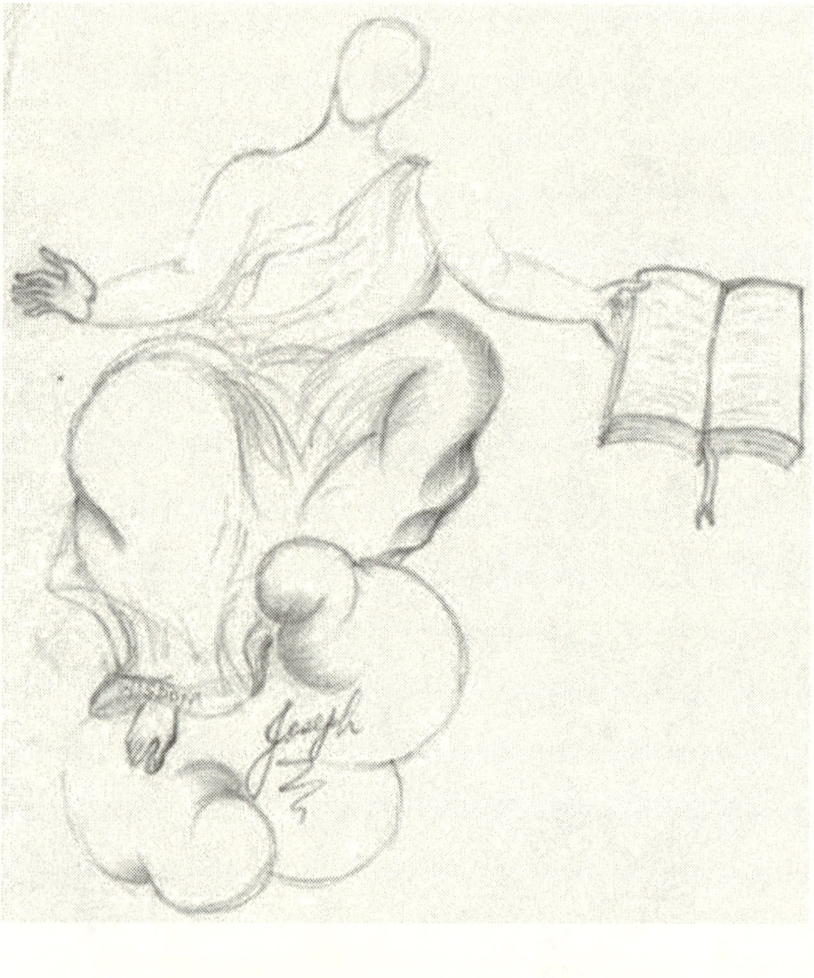

Study of Wisdom-preparatory drawing.

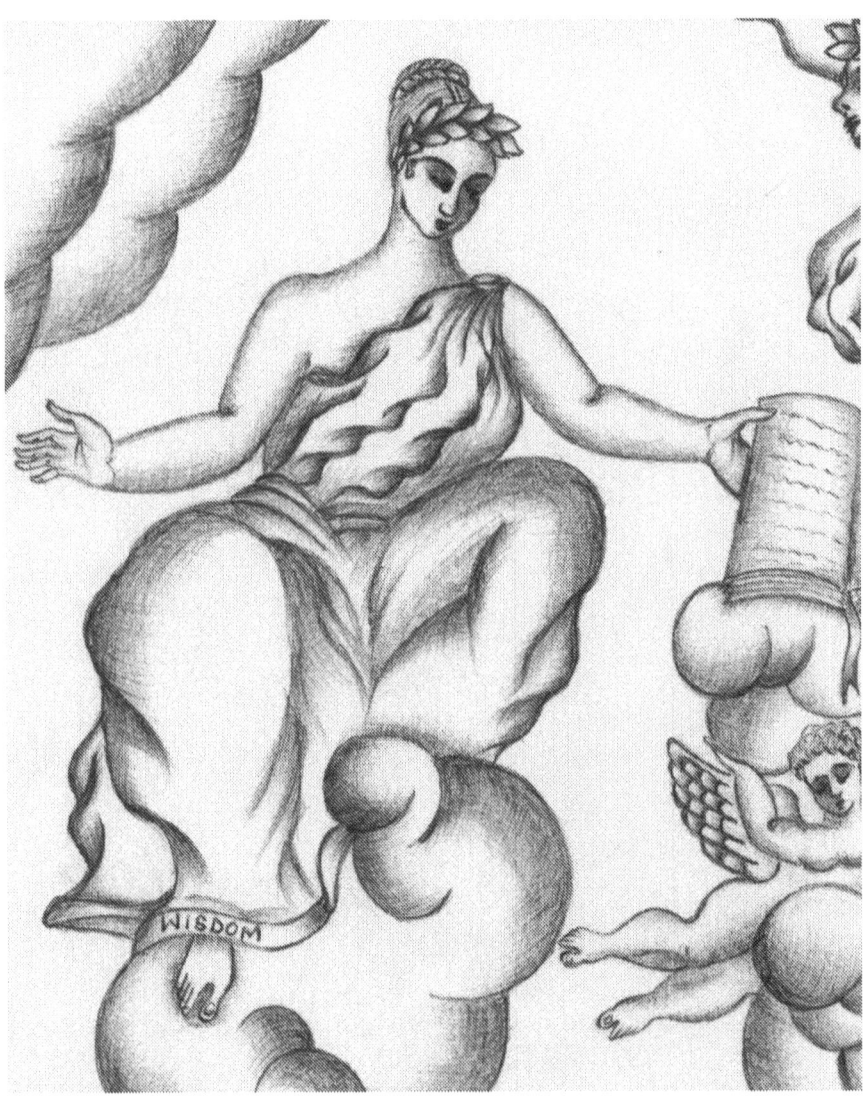

Detail of Wisdom

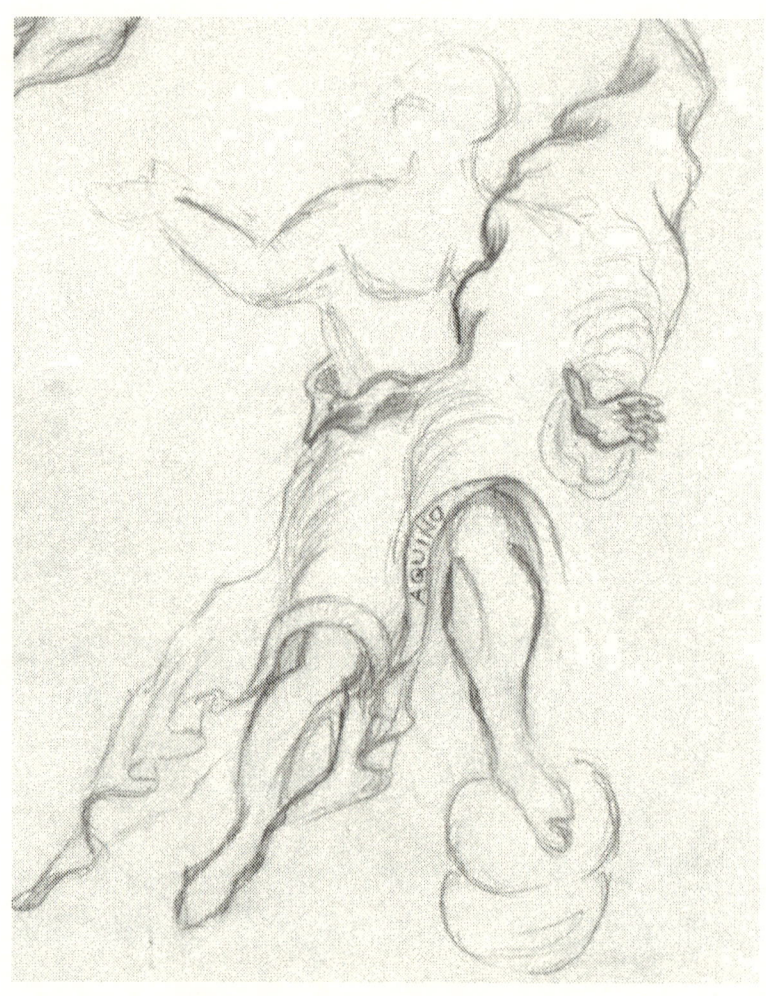

Study of Thomas Aquinas

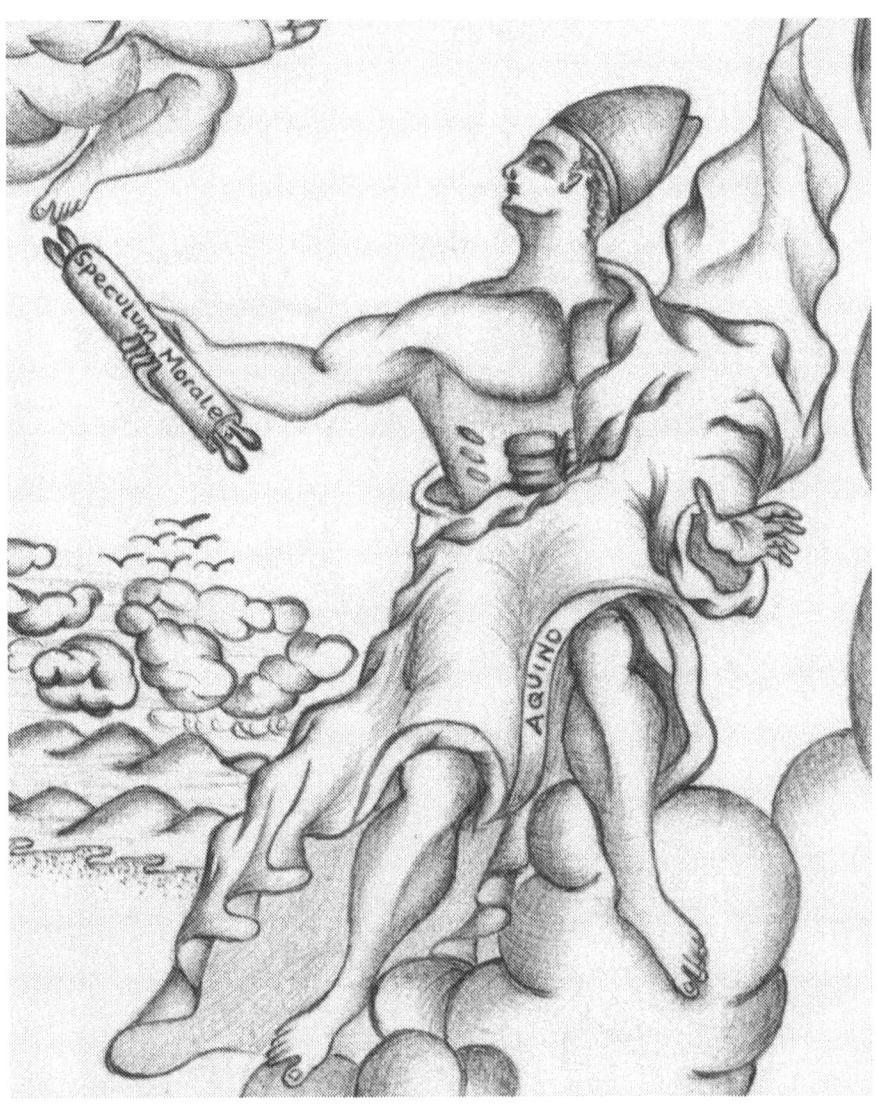

Detail of Thomas Aquinas

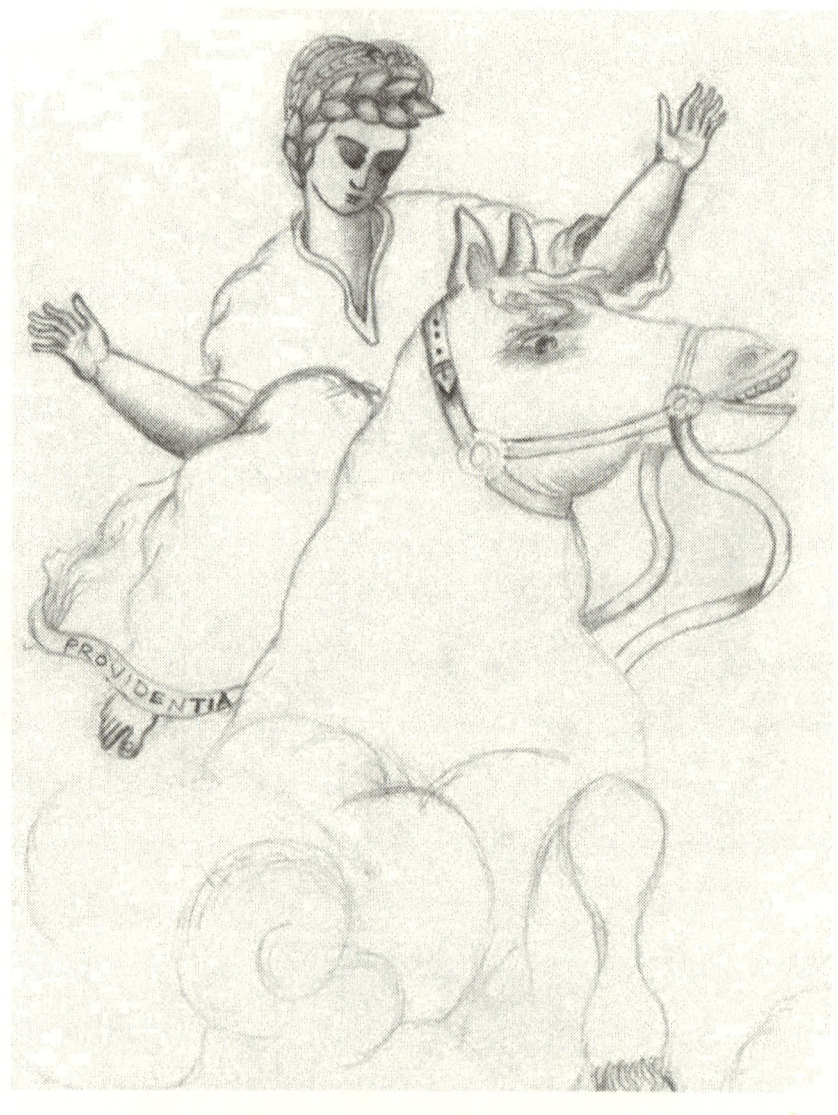

Study of Divine Providence riding a horse
Providence represents *youth* and her *horse* represents *strength*.

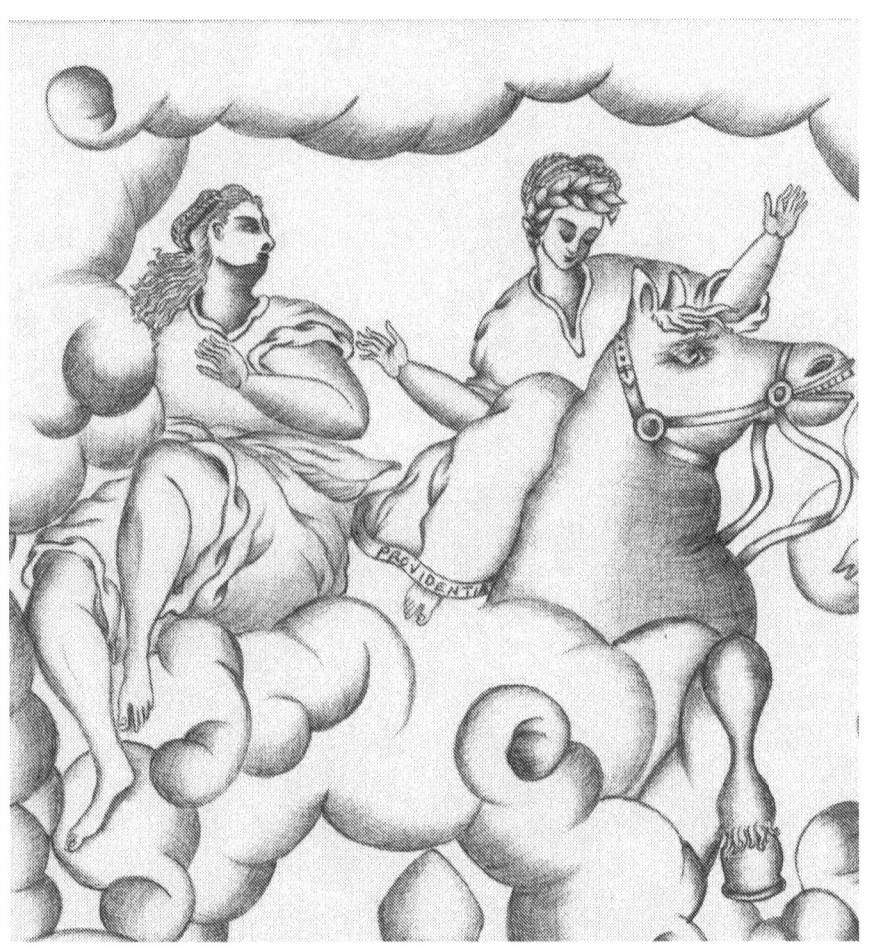

Detail of Prudence and Providence

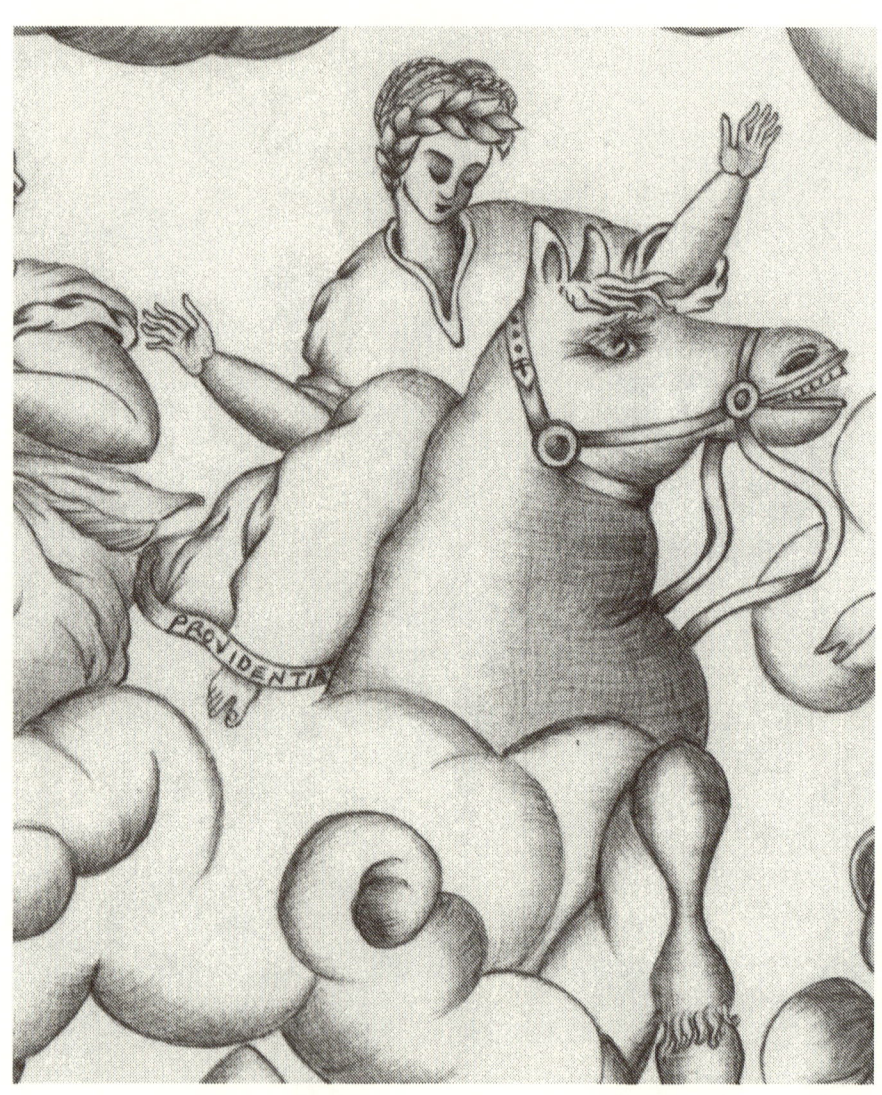

Detail of Providence

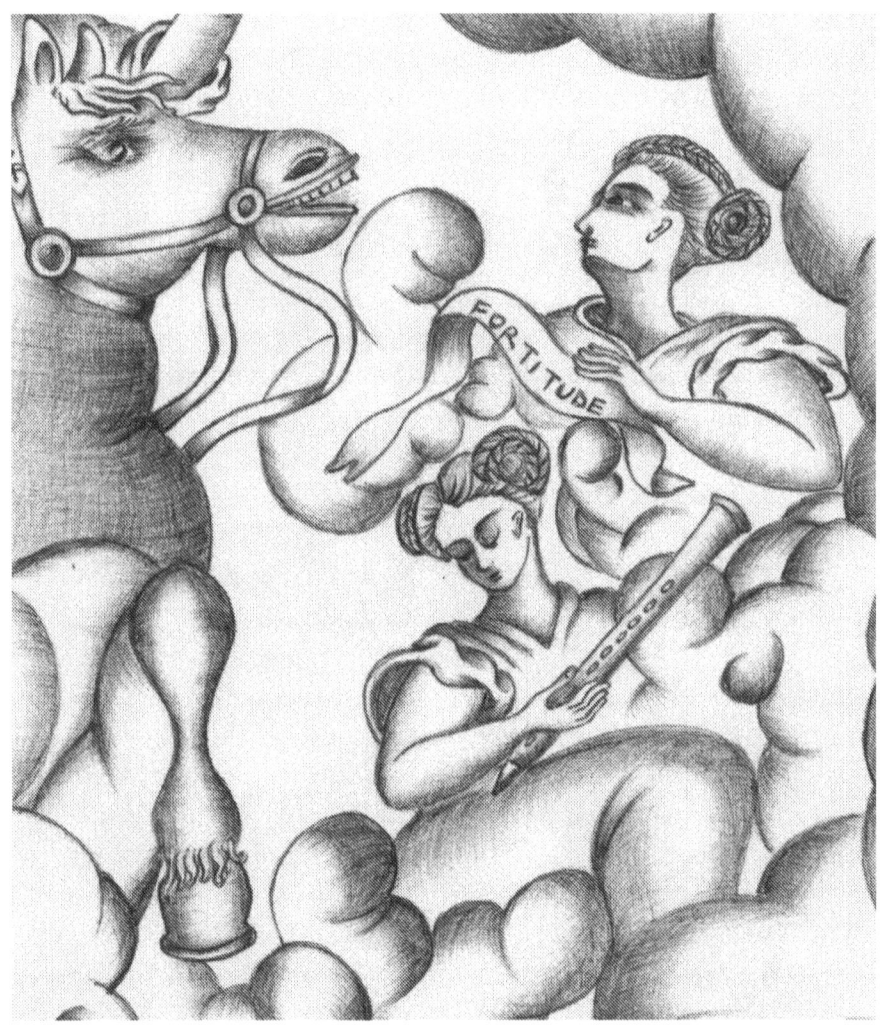

Detail of Fortitude and Temperance

Music and Grammar

The drawings of Music and Grammar are about a love story between the two, who use the liberal arts to express to themselves how they feel about each other. Grammar, the male figure, is on a quest to win Music's heart, who is just as gifted as he is. Grammar uses the written word while Music responds by serenading him with her gift of song.

This lyrical exchange begins when Grammar poses a question to Music, and the two find themselves bound by the yearning that dwells within their hearts. Grammar asks...

...Suppose love, were your lifetime friend?
When you needed a helping hand, it were there to lend
And you had to make a wish, that would forever last
If not companionship, what?

Grammar's question causes a stir within Music, who then decides to travel, in search for a violin because music is the only way through which she can respond. Before she leaves, the two are involved in a duet called *From Heart to Heart.* At the end of the exchange, Music is so lost in the moment, because she knows they will be apart for a while, until she finds a violin. Her piece called *Wandering Thoughts,* tells us how she has been affected by Grammar's presence. The following pages reveal the depth and intimacy of what transpires between the two.

From Heart To Heart
(Both Music and Grammar)

Grammar:

There is a ballad I sing, that I wrote for you
The words you hear, will forever be true
From heart to heart, this is yours from me
Accept it in your life, I ask of thee.

Music:

My precious one, my dearest friend
The sweetest thoughts, to you I send
When you search my heart, you will always find
Special musical notes, that only love can bind.

Grammar:

Oh, Singing Heart, how sweet your sound is
You sing this song, with so much ease
I want you to know, this heart is willing
To receive your sound, for it's so appealing.
When you sing it, do you ever imagine
The number of hearts, that you could win?
Do you think, of the enchantment you bring
To my soul, when I hear you sing?

Music:
Run, my loved one, my arms are open
Moments like these, don't come too often
Both:
We'll both be woven, into a tune so strong
Sing with me, this glorious song.

-Joseph E. Ssali

Wandering Thoughts
(*from Music to Grammar*)

However hard I try
I still don't know why
My thoughts, keep wandering to a place
At such a very fast pace.

I've never been to this place
It's probably out there in space
This happens, when my heart misses you
I'm sure, you've experienced it too.

Some thoughts fade easily, like shades of gray
And yet others, just decide to stay
It all begins, with a simple stare
Before you know it, you're lost in air.

These wandering thoughts, can be distracting
Especially when your mind, begins reacting
You start to think, of the one you miss
And you feel you've lost, your inner-peace.

For wandering thoughts, there is no cure
They grab your heart, like a fish on a lure
When someone you miss, is far away
These thoughts on your mind, begin to stray.

-Joseph E. Ssali

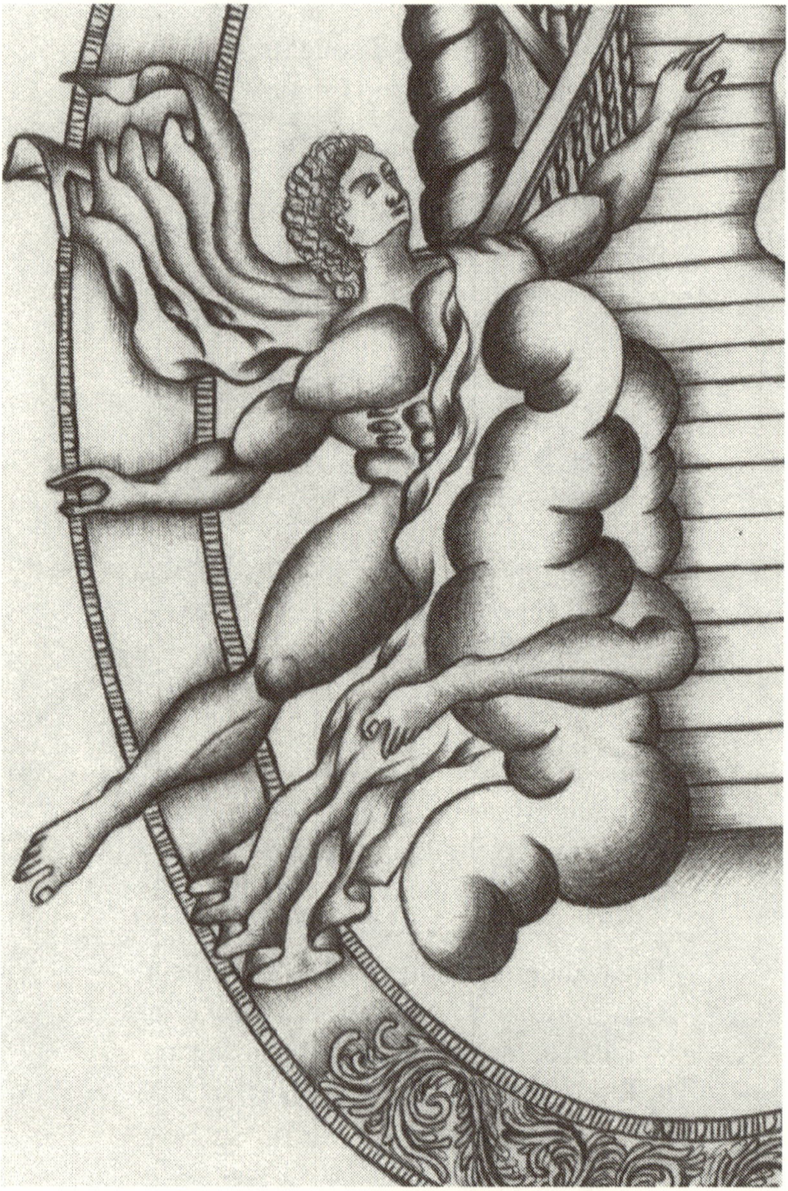

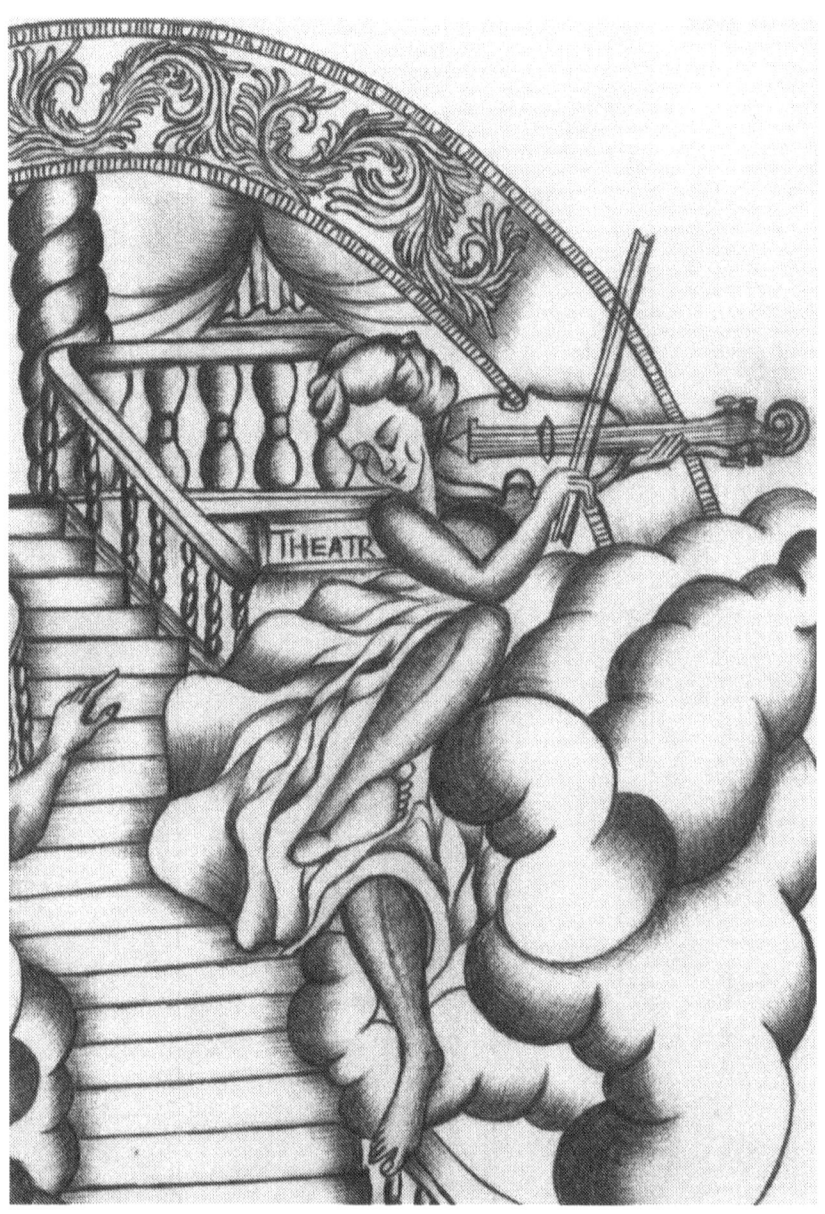

Detail of Grammar on previous page and detail of Music above

PART III

Glossary

African Lion (Latin. Panthera leo)
The most social of all cats, the lion is distributed widely throughout sub-Saharan Africa, and is admired for its strength, courage, loyalty, and nobility. The male lion's mane, which increases with age, adds grandeur to this ferocious cat, and serves to visually intimidate other lions. It also protects the lion's throat against lethal bites during a fight.

Allegorical (Greek, *Allegoria*)
To say something that has hidden meaning that transcends the literal text. A symbolic representation or expression mostly used in paintings, sculpture and architecture in the Renaissance and Baroque.

Arithmetic (Latin. *Arithmetica*, Greek. *Arithmetike*)
A discipline of mathematics that deals usually with numerical expression and with application of the operations of addition, subtraction, multiplication, and division of the same.

Astronomy (Latin. *Astronomia*)
The study of the stars and planets in the atmosphere of the universe and of their physical and chemical properties.

Ballad (Latin. *Ballare*)
An epic or narrative composition in verse, suitable to be set to song, or a popular song especially a romantic or sentimental song.

Baroque (Portuguese. *Barroco*)
The period of time that dates back to the 17th century, that is characterized by the use of complex forms, ornate decor, and the use of contrasting themes, often exhibiting a sense dramatic movement, dynamic energy, and emotionalism. Mostly used in music, art, and architecture.

Basilica (Greek. *Basilike from basilikos*)
An ancient Roman oblong building ending in a semicircular tribune especially used for public assembly, but later on used as the standard architectural form of the early Christian churches.

Bernini (Giovanni Lorenzo Bernini 1598-1680)
This child prodigy was considered a master carver by age eight. Painter, sculptor, poet, and architect, he dominated Rome's artistic scene for over half a century. No other artist left such an imprint on the Eternal City, and Bernini the impresario is responsible for Rome's current appearance. One of his most famous works is The Ecstasy of St. Theresa.

Charity (Latin. *Caritas*)
The most beautiful of all virtues. Generosity and unconditional love shown to those in need. Benevolence and the love of humanity.

Cherubim (Greek. Cheroub, Hebrew. Kerubh)
The second highest rank of angels in the celestial hierarchy. The highest in the celestial order are seraphim. Cherubs and seraphim are the closest to God and are always in His presence. The celestial hierarchy, beginning with the highest ranking, is in the following

nine orders: seraphim, cherubim, thrones, dominions, virtues, powers, principalities, archangels, and angels.

Celestial (Latin. *Caelestis*)
The realm of the atmosphere that is associated with the heavens.

Classical Period (Latin. *Classicus*)
A period of time dating back to the fifth century in Greece where the works exemplified excellence, and were of the highest quality. These included literal, artistic, and architectural masterpieces, including the Parthenon one of the greatest Greek monuments.

Contrapposto (Engl. *Counter-pose*)
To pose in a contrasting position, where one part of the body is turned in a direction opposite the other. Mostly used in Greek classical antiquity and Renaissance, but perfected by the Baroque virtuosos.

Corinth
An ancient cosmopolitan Greek city, and the capital of the Roman province of Achaia. Corinth was noted for its thriving commerce, proud culture, hedonism, and variety of religions.

Dialectic (Latin. *Dialectica*, Greek. *Dialektike*)
Reasoning, discussing and debating by the use of dialogue to explore and expose intellectual beliefs or internal ideas.

Dante Alighieri (1265–1321)
Famous for his Divine Comedy, Dante was a prose writer and moral philosopher who was born in Florence. Another one of his works was *Vita Nuova* (New Life).

Epistle (Latin. *Epistula,* Greek. *Epistole*)
A dignified and gracefully written composition normally in form of a letter.

Faith (Latin. *Fides*)
To hope for that which the human eyes can't see, with a firm conviction that it will come to pass. One of the seven virtues associated with Hope and Love.

Four elements (Latin. *Speculum naturale*)
The natural substance that is celebrated in art. These are: water, wind earth, and fire.

Fortitude (Latin. *Fortitudo*)
To have courage and strength in mind, when faced with danger, adversity or pain. One of the seven virtues, originally celebrated as one the four virtues.

Galleria Borghese (Engl. *The Borghese gallery*)
Known for its rare collections of ancient art and sculpture, this gallery remains one of the most prominent ones in Italy. It was founded by Cardinal Scipione Borghese, the papal nephew, who was from one of Rome's most powerful families during the High Renaissance and Baroque. The three prominent families were: The Baberini family, the Borghese family and the Pamphilj family.

Geometry (Latin. Geometria)
A discipline in mathematics that has to do with the study and relationships of points, lines, angles, circles, surfaces, and solids. It is also one of the seven liberal arts.

Grace (Latin. *Gratia*)
Unmerited special favor bestowed upon man, by God. One of the celebrated virtues.

Grammar (Latin. *Grammatica*, Greek. *Grammatike*)
One of the seven liberal arts, which entails the study of words and their meaning, including the structure of a sentence and syntax of a language.

Gregory the Great, pope (540–604)
Credited with the Gregorian Chant, St Gregory the Great is known for his profound literary works and introduced three more virtues to the original four.

Hope (Latin. *Spes*)
To desire or yearn for something with the expectation of fulfillment. One of the seven virtues often associated with Faith and Love.

Horace (Quintus Horatius Flaccus 65BC–8 BC)
Roman lyric poet and satirist famous for his Odes and verse Epistles that pertain to love, pleasures of friendship, simple life, and the art of poetry. He was the one that made the phrase *'carpe diem'* (seize the day) popular.

Intermediate (Latin. *Intermedius*)
Between two points or realms. The intermediate realm occurs between the celestial and the earthly realm.

Justice (Latin. *Justitia*)
Being impartial and exercising fair judgment, also conforming to truth. Justice is one of the original four cardinal virtues.

Lance (Latin. *Lancea*)
A spear used as a weapon by knights, Vikings, or Roman centurions. The Holy Lance was the spear that was plunged into Christ, in His right side.

Liberal Arts (Latin. *Artes Liberales*)
Disciplines in art whose purpose is to train the freeman. The seven liberal arts are: Grammar, Oratory, Dialectic, Arithmetic, Music, Geometry, and Astronomy.

Logic (Latin. *Logica*, Greek. *Logike*)
The science or branch of knowledge that deals with reasoning.

Longinus St.(It. Longino)
The soldier who plunged a spear in the side of Christ. It is said that some of the blood and water mixture fell in his eyes and he regained his full eyesight. He then abandoned his military post and served in the Christian church. Later on when Emperor Tiberius Caeser heard of this, he ordered his head to be cut off and Longinus died a martyr.

Lucretius (Titus Lucretius Carus 99BC–55 BC)
Roman poet and author of the epic De Rerum Natura (On the Nature of Things).

Martial Eagle (Latin. *Hieraaetus bellicosus*)
A bird of prey that belongs to the raptor family. The Martial Eagle is the largest of all African eagles and is capable of catching a young buck.

Mea Culpa (Engl. *Through my fault*)
A formal admission of one's fault or mistake. Admitting one's bad judgment or personal shortcomings.

Mercy (Fr. *Merci*)
Extending leniency or kindness to the offender. Mercy is one of the virtues that emanates from Divine Love or Charity. Charity is the embodiment of four more virtues which are: Grace, Mercy, Clemency and Leniency.

Metamorphosis (Greek. *Metamorphosis*)
A supernatural change in physical form or state, and the final state is permanent.

Music (Latin. *Musica*, Greek. *Mousike*)
The art of producing harmonious sounds and tones with rhythm, melody and continuity. Music is one of the seven liberal arts.

New Life (Latin. *Vita Nuova*)
Dante's first book that was written by him about his love for Beatrice, the woman whom he fell madly in love with and remained loyal to all his life. It is believed he was inspired to pursue writing after his life was changed by her.

Ode (Greek. *Oide*)
A complex song or lyric poem that is epic in nature and has variation in style, stanza form, and verse.

Oratory (Latin. *Oratoria*)
The art of communicating eloquently using speech-to appeal to the emotions of the listener, mostly done in public.

Ovid (Publius Ovidius Naso, 43BC–17AD)
He was considered to be the most popular poet of his day and is famous for the Metamorphoses.

Providence (Latin. *Providentia*)
The supernatural and divine power of God that guides and sustains human destiny. Divine Providence is fueled by Divine Love and Divine Wisdom.

Prudence (Latin. *Prudentia*)
To govern and discipline oneself with reason, in speech, and actions. One of the seven virtues.

Raconteur (Fr. *Raconteur*)
A person who is highly skilled in the art of telling short narratives of interesting or bewildering incidents, that captivate the listener or intended audience.

Renaissance (Latin. *Renasci*, Fr. *Renaistre*)
The period in Europe between the 14th century and 17th century in which there was a rebirth of knowledge. This intellectual and artistic revival manifested itself in art, music, literature, and architecture.

Sacred (Latin. *Sacrare*)
To cherish something as holy, and to set it aside for divine purposes.

Temperance (Latin. *Temperantia*)
To moderate oneself in thought, action, and emotions. One of the seven virtues.

Time (Latin. *Temporis*)
The allegorical father of Truth. A chronological period in which an event occurs, normally measured in seconds, minutes, and hours.

Trinity (Latin. *Trinus*)
The threefold state of God the Father, God the Son, and God the Holy Spirit, celebrated in the Christian beliefs.

Truth (Latin. *Veritas*)
To have pure intentions and sincere actions. Truth is another one of the virtues, and is often associated with time.

Urban VIII pope (Urbinus Baberinus 1568-1644)
Known as Maffeo Baberini, pope Urban VIII was a patron of the arts and was a poet too. He was born in Florence in the powerful Baberini family. One of his protégés was the great GianLorenzo Bernini who left an imprint of the pope in his works throughout Rome.

Vices (Latin. *Vitium*)
One's shortcomings as a result of moral corruption. The seven vices are: Anger, Envy, Gluttony, Greed, Pride, Lust, and Sloth.

Virgil (Pubilius Vergilius Maro, 70-19 BCE)
Hailed as one of the greatest Roman poets, Virgil is most famous for his piece of writing the Aeneid

Virtues (Latin. *Speculum morale*)
To uphold and live by a certain moral standard. The seven cardinal virtues are: Prudence, Fortitude, Temperance, Justice, Faith, Hope, and Charity (Divine Love).

-END-

0-595-28236-9

www.ingramcontent.com/pod-product-compliance
Lightning Source LLC
Chambersburg PA
CBHW030852180526
45163CB00004B/1547